GEARS OF WAR

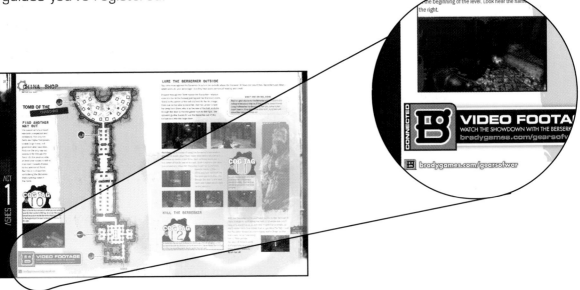

Connecting your BradyGames Connected Guide is easy and can be done in 4 simple steps.

1 To log in, go to BradyGames.com. If you are new to BradyGames, you can join here, as well.

2 Once you're logged in, use the web address provided at the bottom of this page to access the landing page.

3 Register your book by entering the ISBN in the field provided and click Submit. The ISBN is located on the back cover, in the lower right hand corner. It is the ten-digit number labeled ISBN.

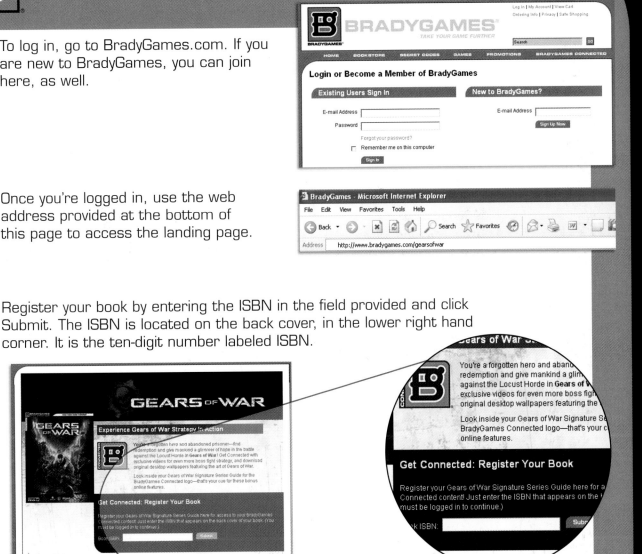

4 Look for the "Access to protected content" link next to your newly registered BradyGames Official Strategy Guide. Click on this link to get your BradyGames Connected content!

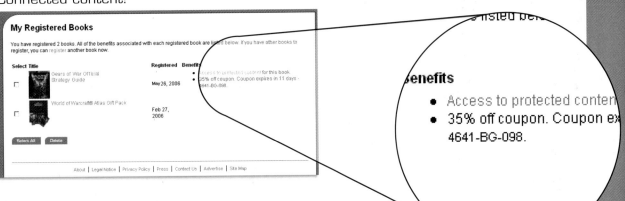

INTRODUCTION

IT'S BEEN FOURTEEN YEARS SINCE THE GROUND FIRST RUMBLED AND CRACKED.
Fourteen long, terrifying years since the Locust Horde emerged from within the heart of the planet and made their insatiable hunger for destruction and death known to the world. Billions of innocent people—men, women, and children alike—have been slaughtered without prejudice. Entire cities have been leveled, armies annihilated, and governments toppled. Finally, with no further options, the Coalition of Ordered Governments assembled their arsenal and unleashed hell upon the planet's surface in an attempt to deprive the Locust of whatever it is they wanted.

And still they came...

After fighting the Locust Horde for over a decade, a highly decorated soldier by the name of Marcus Fenix had gotten wind that his father, a scientist at nearby East Barricade Academy, may be in harm's way. With little time to follow the proper military channels, he made the decision to abandon his squad and try to rescue his father before the Locust onslaught. He was too late. News of Private Fenix's desertion spread rapidly through the ranks to the desk of Colonel Victor Hoffman who took the offense as a personal insult. The panel presiding over the ensuing court martial took little sympathy on Marcus and, under the urging of Colonel Hoffman, blindly overlooked Marcus' superlative military record. He was promptly charged with dereliction of duty and sentenced to 40 years in prison.

Gears of War takes place four long years after Marcus' ramrod trial at the House of Sovereigns. The Locust Horde has finally cracked through the stiff granite bedrock underlying the area surrounding Jacinto Maximum Security Penitentiary, and everyone has been evacuated. Everyone except Marcus, that is. Fortunately for Marcus, his good friend Dominic Santiago hasn't forgotten about him and has come to break him out before the Locust attack. Dominic knows the COG soldiers are in an uphill battle and risks Hoffman's wrath by freeing him. The way Dominic figures it, his Delta Squad could use all the muscle they can get.

As Marcus Fenix, you will experience thirty—six hours in the life of an elite COG soldier. Your mission is one of grave importance and almost impossible odds. Colonel Hoffman has requested that Delta Squad secure a three—dimensional map of the underground Locust network. Armed with this information, it is the COG's hope that they could release a large enough bomb underground to exterminate the Locust Horde once and for all. This is your mission. It might be foolhardy and it may even be impossible, but it sure beats rotting away in solitary confinement.

COALITION OF ORDERED GOVERNMENTS

DELTA AND ALPHA SQUADS

MARCUS FENIX

Son of famed military scientist Adam Fenix, Marcus established a reputation as a brilliant soldier during the Pendulum Wars, earning numerous field promotions and decorations. He was on a fast track to an outstanding military career—until the war with the Locust Horde.

When the Horde breached Jacinto Plateau's defenses, Marcus defied orders so he could save his father. He was too late. Marcus was charged with dereliction of duty and was sentenced to 40 years in Jacinto Maximum Security Penitentiary.

Four years into his sentence, the Horde overtook the penitentiary but Marcus was rescued by his best friend, Dominic Santiago, so that he could rejoin the fight against the unstoppable Locust Horde.

COALITION
OF ORDERED
GOVERNMENTS

Dom is a vocal, colorful, and yet practical soldier. He's loyal to a fault, especially to his friends, and has no patience for those that think of themselves first.

Dominic has always believed in his country and his leaders, but his faith has been slipping in the face of this endless war. Dom lost his wife in the Emergence Day cataclysm. For him, the fight against the Horde is deeply personal.

By testifying in Marcus' defense, Dom prevented an execution, but was forced to accept the heavy judgment the military tribunal handed down to his childhood friend. Never forgetting, Dom seized his first opportunity to save Marcus' life, and convinced Lieutenant Minh Young Kim to enlist Marcus into his squad.

DOMINIC SANTIAGO

Lieutenant Kim is a proud, dedicated and ambitious soldier, a by-the-books believer in all things COG. To Kim, the Coalition of Ordered Governments is humanity's only hope for survival, and he feels that it's an honor and privilege to serve as a Gear.

Kim moved quickly through the ranks, but after a run of bad luck he was left leading the misfits of Delta Squad. Feeling undervalued and overlooked, Kim has something to prove.

Only the strength of Dom's faith— and the scarcity of experienced soldiers—convinced Kim to consider bringing former prisoner Fenix into his squad.

MINH YOUNG KIM

Cole, a.k.a. "The Cole Train," is an adrenaline junkie and former professional thrashball player. He craves action and prefers to take the most direct path to the Locust Horde in any situation. What he lacks in finesse he makes up for in raw energy.

Along with his child-like enthusiasm and charm, Cole is supremely confident in his own abilities to overcome anything, regardless of the odds—and he hasn't been proven wrong yet.

Cole and Damon Baird have served together for years, and he treats Baird as he would an older brother...with a younger brother's license to torment.

AUGUSTUS COLE

COALITION
OF ORDERED
GOVERNMENTS

Despite being a reluctant and cynical soldier, Baird excels in military life. Baird is perfectly capable of being a successful officer, but has never been promoted due to his poor attitude, short temper, and his unwillingness to take on any responsibility.

Baird's greatest strength is his intelligence. He not only fights the Locust, but he studies and observes them as well. He's the closest the COG has to an expert, and when Baird tells his comrades to be quiet and listen, they know it is in their best interest to do exactly that.

Baird's only motivation is self-preservation. He's willing to do whatever it takes to get through the war alive—even march alongside a troublemaker like Fenix.

DAMON BAIRD

SUPPORTING PERSONNEL

The soothing and knowledgeable voice emanating from Delta Squads' earpieces is that of Anya. Anya works for Command Control within COG and is charged with relaying vital information to the units in the field. Her primary role is to monitor the situation and provide strategic advice when needed.

ANYA

JACK

Jack follows the members of Delta Squad everywhere they go, albeit invisibly. This hovering, robotic assistant's primary function is to help with heavy steel doors that must be hot-cut by Jack's blowtorch. Jack is also capable of setting up communication links, downloading data, and transmitting info back to Command Control.

COLONEL HOFFMAN

Colonel Hoffman has seen his fair share of wars and has worked alongside a number of good men. As far as he is concerned, Marcus isn't one of them. Hoffman's strict adherence to military procedure was what landed Marcus in prison, but his inability to forgive and forget is what kept him there.

COALITION
OF ORDERED
GOVERNMENTS

LOCUST HORDE

Locust Drones are the most common enemies in Gears of War. They generally attack in groups of three or four and rely heavily on the Hammerburst and Lancer weapons. Drones use cover and try to keep a safe distance from their foes. As their name implies, Drones are among the less intelligent of the Locust Horde and rarely seek to flank or use sophisticated battle tactics. They prefer to attack en masse and hope their sheer numbers win the day.

You can deal with Drones any number of ways, depending on how many there are and the situation. It's often very easy to flank around a Drone's side and get a clean shot or a chainsaw opportunity. Despite their relative shortcomings, Drones are accurate marksmen. It's imperative to use cover when you deal with them, else you'll get riddled with gunfire.

DRONE

CASUAL	HARDCORE	INSANE
250 HP	550 HP	650 HP

* Note that Locust Spotters and Locust Gunners are identical to Locust Drone units, but are always in close proximity to a Troika. Gunners wear helmets, making head-shots significantly less effective.

These burly creatures are far more aggressive than the Drones. Armed with the Gnasher and Frag Grenades, they can inflict severe damage from close range. Grenadiers aren't the most intelligent creatures, and they occasionally rush forward, hurdling objects in their path and foregoing cover in their rush to kill.

The element of surprise definitely works well for Grenadiers, as they often attack alongside other enemies, such as Drones, Boomers, or Wretches. They appear suddenly and move quickly to get within blasting range. The key to besting them is to recognize their intent and either toss a Frag Grenade in their path or retreat to cover and use the Lancer or Longshot's range to your advantage.

GRENADIER

* Some Grenadiers are outfitted with chest armor. Although they differ from their shirtless counterparts in appearance, they possess the same health and employ the same tactics.

CASUAL	HARDCORE	INSANE
250 HP	550 HP	650 HP

Snipers are very similar to Drones in appearance, but they have far less health and they never engage Marcus at close-range. Instead, Snipers seek out a distant vantage point from which they can shoot with little chance of being seen. Snipers are rather rare, but they are not to be taken lightly. Their bullets pack a terrific punch, and a single head-shot can be enough to down Marcus or an ally. Snipers often occupy the windows or ledges of abandoned buildings.

Snipers are masters of using cover. Combine that with their distant vantage points and you get an enemy that's very difficult to eliminate without using the Longshot weapon. While you can kill some Snipers with the Lancer or even a Frag Grenade, many require accurate sniping. Still, there are other ways to eliminate Snipers, such as using the environment to your advantage. You'll get the chance to unleash the Kryll on them (by shooting out nearby lights). Other methods include detonating nearby propane tanks or collapsing concrete slabs onto them.

SNIPER

CASUAL	HARDCORE	INSANE
75 HP	150 HP	150 HP

No army is complete without a tank, and the Locust Horde is no exception. Enter the Boomer! The Boomer is a hulking, slow-moving beast with an amazing resistance to damage and firepower befitting its size. But the Boomer is far from invincible. This rather dimwitted creature is unconcerned with cover, and he even prefaces each Boomshot blast by yelling, "Boom!" Fortunately for Marcus and his allies, Boomers rarely appear in groups.

Once you spot a Boomer, take cover immediately. From behind cover, lob a Frag Grenade toward the Boomer to weaken him. Continue attacking until he yells "Boom!" Then duck or dive out of the way—as long as the Boomshot's projectile doesn't detonate directly next to Marcus, he should escape without suffering significant splash damage. Focus your team's firepower on the Boomer to down him as quickly as possible. Lastly, resist the urge to attack the Boomer with a melee attack. The chainsaw bayonet does not work against this massive foe, and getting hit with his crushing blow is almost certain death.

BOOMER

CASUAL	HARDCORE	INSANE
1750 HP	2500 HP	2500 HP

Theron Guards are the Locust Horde's ultimate foot soldiers. These large, leather-clad units are superior to Drones and Grenadiers in every way, from intelligence to weaponry. They are masterful Torquebow users. They utilize cover effectively and work together to suppress and flank nearby COG units. In addition to being much more cunning on the battlefield and possessing a weapon that can blow a COG to pieces from long distance, Theron Guards are quite resilient against damage. A single head-shot or burst of machinegun fire won't bring one down.

Approaching a Theron Guard in battle is not something to take lightly or try alone. Use Frag Grenades to draw its attention or flush it out of cover. Allies should provide adequate cover fire for Marcus to move into a flanking position. If they can't, maintain a safe distance and use the Torquebow or Longshot to put down the foe from afar. But beware their Torquebow arrows! Stay behind cover and look for the orange, glowing arrowhead—this is the telltale sign that the Theron Guard is about to fire in your direction. Duck for cover immediately. If Marcus gets hit with a Torquebow arrow, all is not lost. He might survive the resulting explosion if he performs a roll while the arrow detonates.

THERON GUARD

CASUAL	HARDCORE	INSANE
350 HP	800 HP	900 HP

These goblin—like creatures clamber up and down walls and across ceilings just as easily as they hop along the floor. They aren't tall, and they possess no weaponry other than their claws and teeth. But they are as threatening as their gun—toting brethren. Their vast numbers make them dangerous. A lone Wretch poses very little danger, but they often attack by the dozen and rapidly close in on Marcus, gnawing and clawing through his armor with lightning speed.

It's definitely to your advantage to avoid looking for cover during a Wretch fight. Instead, keep moving and use the Gnasher to blast the foul beasts as they swarm near. Consider backpedaling in a large circle around the area to keep the Wretches in view. Also, switch to the Lancer or Hammerburst to shoot the Wretches off the ceiling and prevent them from dropping directly on top of you. Lastly, if you find yourself surrounded by Wretches, use your weapon's melee ability then quickly dive to freedom.

WRETCH

CASUAL	HARDCORE	INSANE
75 HP	150 HP	150 HP

Thanks to their exposure to mass quantities of Imulsion, this breed of Wretches is known to be lambent, which, according to Baird, means that they glow. Dark Wretches are otherwise similar to ordinary Wretches in movement and general behavior. The one big exception: they explode after they're gunned down. This feature, combined with their increased health (on Hardcore and Insane difficulty modes), makes them far more deadly than standard Wretches.

Dark Wretches nearly always attack in large numbers. Shoot them with the Gnasher as quickly as possible. As with standard Wretches, it's best to keep moving and backpedal in a large circle as you fire on them. You must repeatedly dive away from the creatures you shoot to avoid getting caught in their blast radii. Although their explosions aren't particularly large, they are potent enough to kill a character that's too close.

DARK WRETCH

CASUAL	HARDCORE	INSANE
75 HP	200 HP	200 HP

LOCUST HORDE

These flying, organic bombs spew forth from Seeders' tail ends and make a beeline for the nearest COG unit or chopper. Although they seem delicate and harmless upon their initial launch, they soon fix their sights on a target and accelerate. They detonate upon contacting their target and inflict heavy—usually lethal—damage.

The Nemacyst's ability to fly and maneuver around cover makes them a significant threat that you should never ignore. Use the Lancer or Hammerburst to destroy Nemacysts as soon as you spot them. Often, this occurs while you're trying to kill the Seeder from whence they came. Alternate your attacks between the Seeder and the Nemacysts. Their low health makes them easy to kill—it takes just a few Lancer bullets to put one down. Obviously, the sooner you kill the Seeder the quicker the Nemacyst threat subsides.

NEMACYST

CASUAL	HARDCORE	INSANE
15 HP	25 HP	25 HP

These massive, crab—like creatures burrow through the ground. Their backsides protrude from the holes they create in order to launch Nemacysts into the air. Seeders have no direct attack ability and are oblivious to your presence even if you walk right up to it—talk about burying your head in the sand! It just keeps spewing Nemacysts into the air, letting them do its dirty work.

With most of their body safely hidden beneath the ground, Seeders don't pose a direct threat other than their Nemacyst spawn. They have an enormous supply of health and an absolute resistance to conventional weaponry. The only way to kill Seeders is to use the Hammer of Dawn. Stand back and fix the targeting reticule on the Seeder's body, and hold the R Trigger until the satellite's energy attack dissipates. Quickly retarget the Seeder and repeat the attack to finish it off.

SEEDER

CASUAL	HARDCORE	INSANE
5000 HP	5000 HP	5000 HP

The Kryll are a species of nocturnal, carnivorous, bat—like creatures that attack in large swarms. They're invincible, thanks to their overwhelming numbers and their ability to devour a human in seconds. Straying into a darkened area after sunset is almost certain suicide, as only the quickest dive back into the light can bring salvation—no amount of firepower can help you!

Aside from the UV Turret (in the chapter titled "Viaducts"), there is no way to defeat the Kryll. Therefore, the only strategy for dealing with them is to stay in the light to avoid encountering them in the first place. However, you can use the Kryll against other Locust enemies! These indiscriminate feasters attack and kill anything caught in the dark—put them to work by shooting out the fluorescent lights near the enemies, and watch as the Kryll do your bidding!

KRYLL

CASUAL	HARDCORE	INSANE
N/A	N/A	N/A

When it comes to sheer size and power, nothing comes close to the Berserker. These she—beasts are incredibly powerful and fast. Unlike other members of the Locust Horde, they can smash through walls and columns with ease. A single Berserker punch delivers instant death. However, all of this power comes at a price; the Berserker is blind. Her lack of sight has given rise to an acute sense of smell and hearing, which she uses to accurately track Marcus' location. The Berserker turns and charges toward any sound she hears. If she's lucky enough to catch her prey, the poor victim will never make another sound.

The Hammer of Dawn is the only weapon that can make the Berserker vulnerable, as indicated when she glows red. In her vulnerable state, you can use any weapon to finish her off. However, you must lure her outside to use the Hammer of Dawn. Stand at the desired location and either fire at the Berserker or rev the chainsaw bayonet to get her attention. She homes in on the distraction, taking a direct path to its source and crashing through anything in her path in the process. Quickly dive to the side and watch as she slams through whatever you need her to hit.

BERSERKER

CASUAL	HARDCORE	INSANE
6500 HP	8500 HP	12000 HP

This enormous creature is one of the most formidable members of the Locust Horde. Armed with a number of death—dealing claws, a bulletproof shell, and the girth and strength that all Locust envy, the Corpser is one of the most frightening sights in Sera. The Corpser uses its many claws to attack its prey with either a single—claw pierce or a multi—claw squash. The Corpser can also use its claws to destroy the floating blocks Marcus stands on when they square off, thereby limiting Marcus' room to maneuver.

There is only one way to defeat the Corpser: one must shoot its soft, unprotected belly to stun it and then follow up with a shot to its mouth as it cries out in pain. Of course, this is easier said than done thanks to its many claws and spontaneous attacks. Only those who find a good position and shoot between its claws will earn the glory of victory.

*Marcus faces the Corpser in battle only once in *Gears of War*. This battle is detailed in the Act 3 section of this guide's "Campaign Walkthrough."

LOCUST HORDE

CORPSER

CASUAL	HARDCORE	INSANE
10000 HP	10000 HP	10000 HP

The Reaver is a large, multi-legged creature that can fly. These beasts of burden are the Locust Horde's principal battlefield conveyance. They can carry a pair of Locust Horde units. All Reavers have a pair of Troikas mounted on their backs. The rear passenger is often a Theron Guard but occasionally is a Drone. Although the Reaver itself is not a threat, its two riders pose a significant risk to Marcus' life.

Taking cover from the barrage of gunfire and, possibly, Torquebow arrows is crucial when you spot a Reaver. Although one can kill its passengers rather than the Reaver itself, it's easier to aim for the larger target. Using the Lancer or a Troika, unload into the Reaver's side, just below the saddle, to shoot it down. The Torquebow can also down a Reaver. A well-aimed arrow can kill a Reaver (and its riders) with a single shot!

REAVER

CASUAL	HARDCORE	INSANE
750 HP	1500 HP	1500 HP

The Locust Horde leader is a hulking beast at one with the Kryll and well protected by an army of Reavers. RAAM's immense size and strength allow him to rip a Troika from its mount and wield it at will, quickly cutting down any enemy in his path. The flock of Kryll that surrounds him serves as a protective barrier, rendering futile any attempts to shoot RAAM. These traits make him the most lethal foe Marcus will ever face.

Defeating RAAM is no small task. Marcus must make the most of the available cover, use his Frag Grenades to scare off the Kryll, and shoot RAAM's unprotected head while his gun is lowered. He must do all of this while he avoids the dark, defends himself against Reaver attacks, and dodges RAAM's mighty chain gun salvos!

RAAM

* Marcus faces RAAM in battle only once in *Gears of War*. This battle is detailed in the Act 5 section of this guide's "Campaign Walkthrough."

CASUAL	HARDCORE	INSANE
3500 HP	5500 HP	7000 HP

ART OF WAR

This chapter is designed to supplement (not replace) the detailed *Gears of War* user manual. It's our goal to provide additional information and gameplay tips to help you get up and running before Dom ever comes knocking on your cell. For information regarding basic gameplay controls and other fundamentals, please consult your user manual.

GAMEPLAY MODES

CAMPAIGN

The main campaign in *Gears of War* can be played alone or with a friend via the included Co-Op mode. The campaign takes place over the course of 36 hours (in the game universe) and is divided into five acts. Each act has between three and eight chapters.

During the campaign, players control Marcus Fenix, but they're also accompanied by as many as three other AI-controlled characters that round out Marcus' squad. Although there are rare instances in which these characters can perish in battle, they primarily get "downed." The player can revive downed characters by running up to them and pressing the X Button. Alternatively, one can watch them revive themselves at the conclusion of the skirmish—when an area is secured, all downed AI squad mates get up.

DIFFICULTY OPTIONS

You can play the main campaign on any of three difficulty modes: Casual, Hardcore, and Insane. We encourage first-time players to at least try things out on Casual until they get a handle on the gameplay. Hardcore mode is perfect for playing through the game on Co-Op, as the enemies have much higher health, exhibit advanced AI, and are more aggressive. Insane mode, available only after you complete the game on Casual or Hardcore, is incredibly difficult. As one developer said, "Every enemy is a threat to Marcus' life and must be taken seriously." The enemies use advanced AI, have very high health, and Marcus and his cohorts have reduced health.

Available Health per Difficulty Setting				
CHARACTER	PLAYER/AI	CASUAL	HARDCORE	INSANE
Marcus	Player	300	300	175
Dom	Co-Op Player	300	300	175
Dom	AI	300	300	175
Lieutenant Kim	AI	450	450	650
Carmine	AI	450	450	650
Cole	AI	450	450	650
Baird	AI	450	450	650
Jack	AI	750	750	750

CO-OP

You can play Co-Op via split-screen on the same Xbox 360, via System Link, or over Xbox Live. When playing Co-Op, the host always plays the role of Marcus and the person joining the game plays as Dom. Players must use teamwork to limit the amount of damage they take, especially when they have to follow separate paths. Getting downed while you and your teammate are separated is a surefire way to fail the mission objective, as your partner will be unable to reach you.

VERSUS

Gears of War features a robust team-based multiplayer mode, which allows teams to battle it out via System Link or Xbox Live—you can also have one-on-one matches via split-screen. There are ten different Versus maps in the initial game release. There are three different gameplay modes: Assassination, Execution, and Warzone. For more information concerning the game's multiplayer aspect, please consult this guide's "Multiplayer" chapter. There you will find maps and tips for every mode and map in the game.

FUNDAMENTALS OF GAMEPLAY

To survive in *Gears of War*, you must master several facets of gameplay that may not be familiar to you:

- *You must thoroughly and completely understand the importance of cover.*

- *You must be at one with the Active Reload System.*

- *You must know how to use the Tac/Com system to effectively control your AI squad mates.*

COVER

Taking cover behind objects, walls, and other obstacles is monumentally important in *Gears of War*. To take cover, press the A Button, which makes your character back up (or crouch) against an object, shielding him from enemies on the other side of the object. You can move while you're in cover; the Left Thumbstick moves the character alongside the object he's using for protection. You can use the Left Thumbstick in conjunction with the A Button to relocate behind a different piece of cover, such as across a doorway or to a nearby wall or object.

From a cover position, players can press the Right Trigger to blindfire their weapons around or over their cover object. Another option is to press the Left Trigger to lean out.

GETTING INTO COVER:

While you press toward a wall or object with the Left Thumbstick, press the A Button to take cover.

MANTLING:

To mantle over your cover object (from a cover position), press forward on the Left Thumbstick as you press the A Button.

EXITING COVER:

To back out of cover and stand up, press the Left Thumbstick away from the cover object.

SWAT TURN:

Take cover alongside a doorway or at the edge of a wall and hold the Left Thumbstick toward another nearby cover position. Press the A Button to make the character spin across the gap and take cover on the other side.

COVER SLIP:

From a cover position, press Left or Right on the Left Thumbstick to move along the cover object to its edge. From there, press forward or diagonally, depending on cover height.

ART OF WAR

ACTIVE RELOAD

Unlike other games, you actively participate in reloading your weapon in *Gears of War*—if you want to. When it's time to reload, you have several choices: you can empty your gun's magazine and let your character reload it; you can tap the Right Bumper at any time to initiate a reload on your own; or you can tap the Right Bumper once to start the reload and a second time to perform an Active Reload.

The Active Reload meter in the upper-right corner has three distinct parts. There's the large portion of empty black space, the small white area, and the somewhat larger gray area. Tapping the Right Bumper begins the reload procedure, sending the white vertical line on its rightward sweep across the meter. The idea is to tap the Right Bumper a second time to stop the meter within white area. This results in a perfect Active Reload, which is nearly instantaneous. Furthermore, the shells added to the magazine flash white for several seconds, indicating an 8% damage increase for those shells. You can chain successful Active Reloads for additional bonuses. If you stop the meter in the gray area, the reload is slightly faster than normal, but you don't get the damage boost. Finally, stopping the meter in the black space results in a failed Active Reload, which one might equate to a gun jam—the reload procedure takes longer than normal.

ACTIVE RELOAD:

Press the Right Bumper to stop the needle within the white square for a Perfect Active Reload, which allows you to reload faster and grants a damage bonus. Stopping the bar in the gray box results in a Normal Active Reload, which speeds reloading but gives no damage bonus.

FAILED ACTIVE RELOAD:

Once the needle passes the Active Reload meter's gray section, let it go all the way to the end. Stopping it in the black results in lost time.

TAC/COM SYSTEM

Gears of War does not reward lone gunmen. As Marcus, you always have at least one other COG soldier with you, and often two or three others. Although the artificial intelligence (AI) of these characters is very sophisticated and seldom requires user input, you may wish to give a specific command from time to time. This ability is available only to squad leaders (Marcus won't have it until he's a squad leader). To do issue a command, hold the Left Bumper (this also reveals objectives) and then press either the Y Button (Regroup), the B Button (Cease Fire), or the A Button (Attack). Use these commands to make those under Marcus' command gather around him, take cover and hide, or rush the nearest enemy, respectively.

TAC/COM:

These circular icons show your teammates' locations relative to your position. If they're red, it means the corresponding character is currently downed. The TAC/COM circle is more transparent the further away you are from your teammate. This tells you in Multiplayer if it is worth risking a revival, as your teammate could be across the full length of the map.

HEALTH AND DAMAGE

Gears of War does not have a traditional health bar. Nor does it have health packs or first aid kits that you must find in order to heal your player. The red gear that appears in the center of the screen alerts players that their character is suffering damage. The gear's shading gets more intense as the character continues to take damage until he is finally downed. Taking cover, fleeing the action, or neutralizing the threat are viable ways to limit damage. Once the character stops taking damage, the red gear fades just as gradually as it appears, and the character eventually returns to full health.

If the gear get fully red and the player gets downed in a single-player game, the mission is considered failed and the player has to restart. In a Co-Op game, a player can revive his downed partner.

DAMAGE INDICATOR:

A fully red gear like this means your player is about to get downed. Run away, take cover, or neutralize the threat, then wait for the gear to fade away.

WEAPONRY

Players can carry up to four different weapon types at any given time, but certain limitations dictate which four can be carried simultaneously. Use the Directional Pad to access the Weapon Switcher—tap either left, right, up, or down to pick from the available weapons.

WEAPON SWITCHER:

The upper slot is reserved for grenades, the left and right slots are for two-handed weaponry, and the bottom slot stores pistols.

TWO-HANDED WEAPONS

Players can carry up to two different two-handed weapons at a time. We recommend keeping the Lancer or Hammerburst in the right slot and using the left slot for other weapons, such as the Gnasher or the Longshot.

ART OF WAR

LANCER

Lancer Statistics

USER	CASUAL DAMAGE	CASUAL MELEE	HARDCORE DAMAGE	HARDCORE MELEE	INSANE DAMAGE	INSANE MELEE
Player	20	N/A	20	N/A	20	N/A
AI	20	N/A	20	N/A	20	N/A

MAGAZINE SIZE	AMMO CAPACITY	RATE OF FIRE	RATE OF RELOAD
60	660	850	2.5

The Lancer is the primary assault rifle of COG soldiers everywhere. This fast-firing rifle is effective at all but the longest range, but it packs the weakest punch. The weapon compensates for this shortcoming with its chainsaw bayonet. Rather than simply bashing an enemy with the butt of the rifle, the Lancer lets you saw an enemy in half! Hold the B Button to rev up the chainsaw bayonet as you approach an enemy, and move within striking range. Note that you're forced to lower the chainsaw bayonet when you get shot.

HAMMERBURST

Hammerburst Statistics

USER	CASUAL DAMAGE	CASUAL MELEE	HARDCORE DAMAGE	HARDCORE MELEE	INSANE DAMAGE	INSANE MELEE
Player	28	34	26	31	26	31
AI	30	36	30	36	30	36

MAGAZINE SIZE	AMMO CAPACITY	RATE OF FIRE	RATE OF RELOAD
78	780	1250	2.5

The Hammerburst is the primary Locust weapon. This assault rifle lacks the Lancer's chainsaw bayonet, but makes up for it with greater firepower and a faster firing rate. True to its name, the Hammerburst fires rounds in a burst of six. Holding the R Trigger makes the Hammerburst fire continuously, albeit in a repeating, six-shot "tat-tat-tat, tat-tat-tat" pattern. This helps conserve ammo, as you should rarely hold the trigger for prolonged periods anyway.

GNASHER

Gnasher Statistics

USER	CASUAL DAMAGE	CASUAL MELEE	HARDCORE DAMAGE	HARDCORE MELEE	INSANE DAMAGE	INSANE MELEE
Player	180	216	180	540	180	540
AI	72	86	114	342	114	342

MAGAZINE SIZE	AMMO CAPACITY	RATE OF FIRE	RATE OF RELOAD
8	39	60	3.0

When it comes to close-range firepower, nothing beats the Gnasher! This shotgun-style weapon can blow huge holes in enemies that stray too close. This is a great weapon to use against charging foes with smoking chainsaws. Plus, it's especially easy to fire from the hip, thanks to its wide spread pattern. Although the Gnasher isn't effective at long range, it is truly precious in confined spaces, for dealing with Wretches, and when you're looking to crack skulls in multiplayer mode!

LONGSHOT

Longshot Statistics

USER	CASUAL DAMAGE	CASUAL MELEE	HARDCORE DAMAGE	HARDCORE MELEE	INSANE DAMAGE	INSANE MELEE
Player	350	420	350	420	350	420
AI	150	180	150	180	150	180

MAGAZINE SIZE	AMMO CAPACITY	RATE OF FIRE	RATE OF RELOAD
1	24	60	3.0

The Longshot is the game's designated long-range sniper rifle. It possesses incredible accuracy, devastating firepower, and an exceptional zoom. With the Longshot, a simple click of the Right Thumbstick lets the player zoom in on distant enemies with such precision that picking off a Drone behind the protection of a Troika is almost routine! However, unlike other weapons, the Longshot has room for just a single bullet in the magazine, and it has a relatively slow reload time. Nevertheless, there are few things more deadly than a bullet fired from the Longshot after a perfect Active Reload.

BOOMSHOT

Boomshot Statistics

USER	CASUAL DAMAGE	CASUAL MELEE	HARDCORE DAMAGE	HARDCORE MELEE	INSANE DAMAGE	INSANE MELEE
Player	525	315	525	630	525	630
AI	300	360	400	480	400	480

MAGAZINE SIZE	AMMO CAPACITY	RATE OF FIRE	RATE OF RELOAD
1	6	60	2.5

It seems in every war, there's a weapon that can turn the tide of battle with a single trigger squeeze or button press. In the war against the Locust Horde, one might categorize the Boomshot that way. The Boomshot fires a large projectile, not unlike a rocket-propelled grenade. Upon impact, it explodes into separate, smaller projectiles. Scoring a direct hit with the Boomshot destroys the targeted enemy, rendering its horrendously gutted body unidentifiable. Although the Boomshot carries a low ammo capacity, it's positively deadly as a melee weapon—don't be afraid to hold onto it after you've run out of ammo.

TORQUEBOW

Torquebow Statistics

USER	CASUAL DAMAGE	CASUAL MELEE	HARDCORE DAMAGE	HARDCORE MELEE	INSANE DAMAGE	INSANE MELEE
Player	708	850	708	850	708	850
AI	275	330	380	456	380	456

MAGAZINE SIZE	AMMO CAPACITY	RATE OF FIRE	RATE OF RELOAD
1	12	60	3.0

The Torquebow is arguably the most unusual weapon in Gears of War. This bladed bow fires grenade-tipped arrows with tremendous accuracy at considerable range. It's important to note that the Torquebow does not behave like a firearm, nor should it! To use the Torquebow, use the Left Trigger to Aim (as is normal) and then squeeze and hold the Right Trigger to draw the bowstring, allowing the targeting laser to straighten. You have eight seconds from the time you begin drawing the string until the bow auto-fires. Although tapping the Right Trigger makes an arrow fly a short distance, arrows penetrate their targets only after you hold the bowstring for several seconds.

HAMMER OF DAWN

The Hammer of Dawn is a satellite-based weapon that functions only out in the open and, even then, only when Anya reports that there are satellites overhead. The hand-held apparatus is really just a sophisticated targeting system. When you stand still and fix the Hammer of Dawn's targeting reticule on a solid surface for several seconds, the satellites overhead triangulate the position and open fire with their powerful energy beam. Once the satellites begin firing, you can move the targeting reticule to attack other nearby enemies. The energy beam cuts off after roughly eight seconds, at which time the targeting system must be reset.

PISTOL-TYPE WEAPONS

SNUB PISTOL

Snub Pistol Statistics

USER	CASUAL DAMAGE	CASUAL MELEE	HARDCORE DAMAGE	HARDCORE MELEE	INSANE DAMAGE	INSANE MELEE
Player	50	60	50	60	50	60
AI	50	60	50	60	50	60

MAGAZINE SIZE	AMMO CAPACITY	RATE OF FIRE	RATE OF RELOAD
12	72	700	2.0

The Snub Pistol has a very fast firing rate and adequate power. Its semi-automatic design literally puts the firing speed in your hands—how fast can you pull the R Trigger? The weapon is lightweight, easy to aim, and has a 2x zoom (click the Right Thumbstick) that can definitely ease the task of targeting distant enemies.

BOLTOK PISTOL

Boltok Pistol Statistics

USER	CASUAL DAMAGE	CASUAL MELEE	HARDCORE DAMAGE	HARDCORE MELEE	INSANE DAMAGE	INSANE MELEE
Player	150	180	150	180	150	180
AI	175	210	175	210	175	210

MAGAZINE SIZE	AMMO CAPACITY	RATE OF FIRE	RATE OF RELOAD
6	30	60	2.0

This revolver-type weapon looks a lot more traditional than the Snub Pistol, and its performance is certainly much slower. But it packs a mean punch! The Boltok Pistol features the same 2x zoom of the Snub Pistol, but it possesses enough power to put an enemy down with a single headshot! Equally important, it delivers far more damage than many weapons when one uses it in a melee situation.

GRENADES

FRAG GRENADES

Frag Grenades are the only grenade type you encounter in the main campaign. One can throw them a considerable distance. When you hold the Left Trigger, a tracer line helps you ascertain your throw's trajectory. A Frag Grenade explodes with enough force to kill several enemies within its blast radius. Frag Grenades detonate roughly two seconds after you throw them—they are not proximity bombs. You can tag an enemy with a Frag Grenade by equipping the weapon and hitting the enemy with a melee attack. Just be sure to run away before your "friend" explodes!

SMOKE GRENADES

Smoke Grenades appear only in Multiplayer mode as part of each player's standard issue. Although Smoke Grenades cannot actually harm anyone, they do serve two useful purposes. For starters, players can use them to conceal their movements. If you're caught in a standoff with an enemy unit, throw a Smoke Grenade and relocate without being seen. Like a Frag Grenade, you can also use a Smoke Grenade to tag an opponent. Although this doesn't harm your foe, it humiliates him and alerts everyone to his position for the next 15 seconds or so.

GENERAL GAMEPLAY TIPS & TACTICS

TAKE COVER!

The creators of *Gears of War* have made it clear that they weren't looking to create just another run-and-gun shooter. Cover is the key to success in this game. Running around with guns blazing does little more than get you killed. And, as the difficulty level increases, so does the frequency of the "Objective Failed" screen—that is, unless you use cover to your advantage.

YOU ARE NOT ALONE

Your AI-controlled squad mates are there to provide support and direction as the game advances—be sure to take advantage of their presence. Whenever they are downed, try to revive them as quickly as possible so long as it doesn't put you at unnecessary risk. Your AI partners automatically revive when you reach a new checkpoint, but that might be too late.

UNDERSTAND THE DIFFICULTY SETTINGS

In Hardcore and Insane modes, those who fail to use cover and flank their enemies won't survive long. Casual Mode is more forgiving of those who wander from cover on occasion and attempt frontal assaults when they shouldn't. Hardcore Mode cracks down on this behavior, as damage the enemies inflict and the effort it takes to destroy them is increased. Insane mode requires near perfect observance of the game's ideals and techniques. Cover is a necessity in all firefights,

 but that's not nearly enough. You must watch your flanks and relocate accordingly, as enemy speed and intelligence increases exponentially. Enemies that find you camping too long rush your position; some even hop over your cover and attack with deadly melee techniques. The amount of damage it takes to destroy enemies is significantly higher, and we highly recommend aiming for the head.

PICK UP EVERYTHING YOU CAN

There is usually a generous amount of ammo to be had, so take a moment to collect as much of it as possible. That said, if your weapon is almost full, make a mental note of where extra ammo is located so you can come back for it later. Wasting ammo when you don't really need it is almost worse than not grabbing any at all. Often, an enemy type appears just after a weapon that's particularly effective at killing them becomes available—use this to your advantage!

ART OF WAR

WEAPONS STORAGE SOLUTIONS

Pistols and Frag Grenades are automatically stored in their respective slots when you pick them up. But all other weapons replace the weapon in your hand when you grab them. Remember how you store your weapons so you can quickly switch to the right one for the job at hand. Giving up your Gnasher makes you less effective at short range, but dropping it for a Longshot increases your potency against distant enemies. You have to give to get, so go with what works best for the situation. We recommend always keeping the Lancer (or Hammerburst) in the weapon slot to the right, as switching to this default all-purpose weapon will become second-nature.

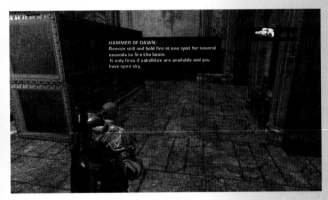

ONLY FOOLS RUSH IN

Never walk past or through an open doorway without first taking cover alongside it and doing a little recon. Try to size up the situation as best you can, and choose a weapon that's suited for the task ahead before you advance. Reload if necessary, and try to scout out your next piece of cover—use the maps in this guide for help!

ACTIVE RELOAD OFTEN, AND PRACTICE IT!

When you face a large firefight ahead, try blindfiring at enemies while you maintain cover, and don't be afraid to exhaust your entire magazine. If you manage to pull off a perfect Active Reload, you're looking at an entire clip of powered-up shots (for a limited duration). This really can help you take down enemies at an accelerated rate. Remember that the flashing bullets in the HUD deliver, on average, 8% more damage than normal bullets.

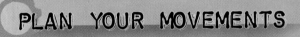

PLAN YOUR MOVEMENTS

You can't take all the time in the world, because the enemy tries to flank you and adjusts to your position, so try to plan ahead where you want to go. React to your squad mates' movements, work the angles to flank the enemy, and force them from cover. Often, squad mates yell for Marcus to flank to a particular side. These guys know their stuff, so follow their advice!

DON'T ASK "Y," PRESS IT!

There are many Points of Interest scattered throughout the campaign that offer a close-up view when you're prompted to press the Y Button. They aren't always critical in terms of Marcus' survival, but they provide information and give you a sense of actually living through the story as it unfolds.

EXPLORE YOUR SURROUNDINGS BEFORE YOU ADVANCE

The best time to search an area for COG Tags or ammo is after a battle ends and the smoke clears. Refer to the COG Tag explanation in this guide's Act 1 Walkthrough. Pay attention to the red Crimson Omen indicators; a little searching is all it takes to find their corresponding COG Tags. Destroy all crates and furniture in your vicinity with the hope of uncovering a hidden COG Tag or extra ammunition. Also, you may have to reenter the room you're in from an alternate entrance in the next area in order to find the COG Tag.

FIRE IN THE HOLE!

Close Emergence Holes as quickly as possible to prevent further enemies from surfacing. Frag Grenades are great for taking out groups of enemies in a firefight, but try to conserve them for sealing the many Emergence Holes that sprout up all around you. Emergence Holes close after you deal with all of the Locusts within them, but using a Frag Grenade is a great way to conserve ammo.

APPROACH SPLIT PATHS AS UNIQUE SITUATIONS

When the path splits, there's a good chance that either you or the other team can provide significant squad support. Such opportunities often come in the form of higher elevations or superior attack angles. Size up the situation to determine who is in the flanking position, and take advantage of it.

ART OF WAR

ACT I: ASHES

ACT 1

ASHES

SITUATION REPORT

A military prison can be an unforgiving place. But as cold and hard as the steel and concrete can feel, it can sometimes pale in comparison to the ruthless, unsympathetic demeanor of the men who run it. This is the hand that has been dealt to one Marcus Fenix, an accomplished soldier who has spent the past several years paying for a single indiscretion any loving son would have made. Charged with Dereliction of Duty for abandoning his post, Marcus has been left to rot—alone—in an otherwise vacant prison. With the Locust Horde on the prison's doorstep, his former commanding officer has pardoned everyone except him. Everyone always knew Marcus was special.

FIRST ENCOUNTERS

DRONE

Drones are the basic Locust grunts, and they attack with limited intelligence. They rely primarily on the Hammerburst weapon, although some will come to possess a Lancer every now and then.

GRENADIER

These bare-chested brutes are very aggressive and excel at short- to mid-range combat, thanks to their supply of Frag Grenades and use of the Gnasher.

SPOTTER

This mask-wearing member of the Locust clan is similar to a Drone but is sent out only to accompany those manning a Troika. It is rarely on the go, as it prefers to stand and alert the gunner to COG Team whereabouts.

GUNNER

For some, using the Troika is a unique opportunity. For the Gunner, it's all he knows. The Gunner is a designated Troika expert and must be flanked to be eliminated.

WRETCH

Wretches are fast, nimble creatures that run across the ceiling en masse and attempt to claw their prey to death. They are unintelligent and very easy to put down.

NEMACYST

These flying, organic bombs are spewed forth from the tail-end of a Seeder and are as deadly as they are putrid. They seem to harmlessly float toward their targets, but explode with deadly power on contact.

SEEDER

These massive creatures seldom leave their equally large Emergence Holes. They attack from afar by spewing a constant barrage of Nemacysts into the air. They can be killed only with the Hammer of Dawn.

BERSERKER

This massive monstrosity can't see, but boy can she smell and hear! Capable of smashing through solid walls and killing humans with a single claw swipe, the Hammer of Dawn is the only way to stop her.

COG
TAGS

01
In the rear of the courtyard, directly across from the cell area.]

02
In the cellblock area, under the stairway on the left-hand side.

03
In the lower southwest corner of the prison yard.

04
On the ground, in the first outer yard area on the way to Embry Square.

05
Hidden amongst the weeds, just beyond the second Emergence Hole that opens in the inner yard.

06
In the far left-hand corner of the plaza, near the large, empty fountain.

07
To the left of the van with the Crimson Omen on it, near the crack in the street.

08
In the hallway with the Wretches, to the far left of the door Jack is opening.

09
Cross the sanctuary and descend the steps into the next room. The COG Tag is behind the beam on the right.

10
Inspect the area where the Berserker killed the soldier at the beginning of the Tomb.

11
The COG Tag is on the floor, to the left of the third door that you need the Berserker to smash.

12
Outside the Tomb. Follow the wall to the left upon exiting, and get the COG Tag before killing the Berserker.

14 YEARS AFTER E-DAY
Time off for good behavior.

JACINTO MAXIMUM
SECURITY PRISON

EXTRACTION POINT

START

x2

01

02

x16

CAMPAIGN WALKTHROUGH

As far as solitary confinement goes, Marcus isn't short on visitors. Fortunately for him, not all his guests today are as unwelcome as the Wretches crawling around atop his cell bars. Marcus' old war buddy, Dom, has come to break him out of prison—he even brought a bag of gear for Marcus, including the **Hammerburst** assault rifle and **Snub Pistol**. The former may not be standard COG issue, but it will do.

EXIT THE CELL AREA

Dom wastes no time deferring to Marcus with regard to escape plans. There are two routes out of the prison: They can either go through the guards' quarters, which is a relatively safe route, or they can take the shortcut through the cellblocks and deal with the Locust that have already entered the area. We recommend that first-time players opt for the easier route to the right.

COLLECT THE 30 COG TAGS

There are 30 COG Tags scattered throughout the *Gears of War* campaign. The more you find, the more Achievements and Gamer Points you'll earn! Although many of the COG Tags are located off the beaten path, every one of them has a corresponding Crimson Omen in the vicinity. Keep your eyes peeled for the spray-painted Crimson Omen insignia, as that is your one surefire clue that a COG Tag is nearby. Some of the COG Tags will be on the floor directly near the Crimson Omen, whereas others are less obvious.

Until Dom calls in to request a pickup, no one is aware that Dom and Marcus are still in the prison and therefore at risk from the air raids taking place. There is a courtyard at the far end of the prison where they can rendezvous. Until then, the twosome is on its own.

COG TAG #01

Cross the courtyard outside the prison cell area toward the rear wall—you can do this regardless of the direction you opt to take when talking with Dom. Locate the COG Tag on the ground in front of the Crimson Omen.

HEAD TOWARD THE GUARDS' QUARTERS

If you choose the right-hand path, continue reading. If you follow the left path, skip to the next section, entitled "Left Path: Combat."

Follow the sign for the cafeteria and ascend the two flights of stairs to the security room above. Grab the ammunition box behind the couch on the right. These boxes contain extra ammo for most every weapon except Frag Grenades, whereas dropped weapons yield ammo that's exclusive to that specific weapon type.

USE THE BUTTON TO OPEN THE SECURITY DOOR

The door across the room is currently locked. Approach the green-lit button on the desk and press the X Button. The X Button is a multi-purpose button used for interacting with objects, kicking doors, picking up items, and even curb-stomping a downed opponent.

SHOOT THE TWO BREAKERS TO UNLOCK THE DOORS

Follow Dom to the locked door on the balcony ahead. A portion of this upper walkway has been destroyed. In order to get to the prison blocks, the duo must first go through the two rooms on this floor. Unlock the doors to these rooms by shooting the circuit breakers near the doors; these control

the locking mechanisms. Use the L Trigger to aim Marcus' weapon and the R Trigger to fire. The circuit breakers have faint red lights—shoot them!

GET TO THE PRISON BLOCKS

Approach the door and press the X Button to kick it open. The vacated room contains several columns and obstacles that are perfect for practicing the art of using cover. Use the A Button in combination with the Left Thumbstick to move in and out of cover, to roll, and to hurdle over a low-lying object. Kick open the door at the end of the second room to return to the balcony. Continue out onto the prison wall on the right.

A low-level Locust unit known as a Drone is holed up inside the guard tower halfway across the walkway. Take cover behind the toppled pillar and use blindfire to take it out. Follow Dom across the wall and press the button in the guard tower to open the security door in the distance. The door will stay open only for a few seconds, so Marcus must Roadie Run in order to get through. Hold the A Button to make him duck forward and run with his head down.

Descend the stairs on the right and gather up the grenades in the room on the right. Follow Dom outside onto the balcony. Really work over the pair of Drones below with Frag Grenades. Don't hesitate to use half a dozen or so, as there's an ample supply. Circle around to the right and descend the stairs to reach the main prison block area.

LEFT PATH: COMBAT

OPEN THE JAMMED DOOR

Approach the door on the left and press the X Button to kick it open. The X Button is a multi-purpose button used for interacting with objects, kicking doors, picking up items, and even curb-stomping a downed opponent.

GET TO THE PRISON BLOCKS

Move into cover behind the toppled column by pressing the A Button while pushing toward the pillar with the Left Thumbstick. From this position, Marcus can blindfire the Drones approaching from the far end of the area. Another way to kill them is to use the L Trigger in conjunction with the Right Thumbstick to manually take aim on the Drones. However, this method exposes more of Marcus' body from cover. Once you've put down the Drones, grab the Frag Grenades on the floor and enter the prison block area up ahead.

Dom helps lure the Drones' attention toward the center of the block. This allows Marcus to slide into cover just beyond the door and take out the Drones on the ground. If you kill one, the other often retreats, allowing you to gun him down as he runs. The trickiest one to get is inside the room at the far side of the area. This room has no roof, so you can easily toss a grenade over the wall. To do so, switch to Frag Grenades by tapping Up on the Control Pad and aiming and firing with the L and R Triggers, respectively.

WELDING DOOR

Don't worry about collecting the ammo and nearby COG Tag just yet; first get behind the piece of cover in the middle of the area and ready a grenade. Hold the L Trigger and aim the grenade's trajectory at the door that's being cut open by the Grunts on the other side. Wait for the door to fall, and throw the grenade to destroy most of the assailants. Finish off any stragglers from behind cover.

FALLEN COMRADES

Dom can be "downed" if he suffers too much damage. Watch for his location icon on the HUD to turn red, as this is the sign that he is severely injured. You can either rush to his aid by pressing the X Button to revive him, or you can squelch the ambush on your own. If you succeed in defeating all the enemies in the area, any downed allies will automatically return to full health. However, if they get executed, you will fail the mission and have to restart from the previous Checkpoint.

COG TAG #02

The COG Tag is on the ground, under the stairway opposite the one you descended if you took the training route. It's to the left and below the Crimson Omen painted high on the wall.

CAMPAIGN WALKTHROUGH

PROCEED TO THE YARD FOR EXTRACTION

Multiple Grunts are waiting in the yard to intercept Dom and Marcus as they attempt to flee. Dom uses the short wall near the yard's entrance for cover while he draws the enemy fire. Marcus must climb the stairs on the left and flank the enemy. Use the cover on the left to take out any Locust that may be on the walkway, and then slide into position near the steps leading back down to the ground. From there, Marcus can swiftly eliminate many of the Locust, either with the primary weapon or with any grenades he still has in hand.

Coalition Command senses an underground disturbance and promptly calls off the counterattack. A lone King Raven chopper is made available for extraction, but you'd better hurry! Grab the COG Tag on the ground to the left and make a dash for the chopper.

The Crimson Omen for this COG Tag is in the lower southwest corner of the yard.

TRIAL BY FIRE

Begin the mission to find Alpha Squad.

EMBRY SQUARE

1 OF 3

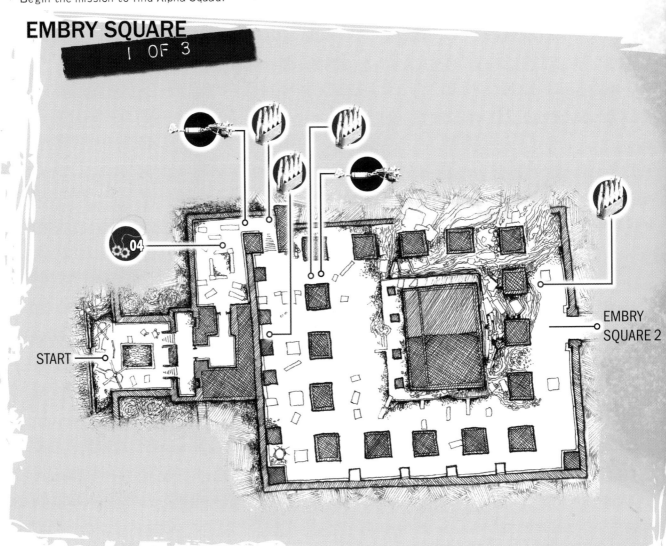

04

START

EMBRY SQUARE 2

SEARCH FOR ALPHA SQUAD

The reunion with Hoffman goes about as well as Marcus could hope for, but the news isn't great—he's stuck here for the time being. Fortunately, Hoffman and Anya hop back into King Raven and crush the initial wave of Locust attackers outside Embry Square.

HOLD ONTO THE LANCER!

As much as Hoffman can't stand Marcus, he knows the ex-con doesn't have a chance against the Locust without the proper weaponry. Marcus is now equipped with the **Lancer**, the legendary assault rifle with a chainsaw bayonet. This weapon is extremely useful in all types of situations, so be careful when picking up ammunition and weapons—do *not* accidentally swap out the Lancer.

Ascend the stairs alongside Carmine, Dom, and Lieutenant Kim, and regroup near the entrance. Proceed down the corridor toward the yard outside, and allow your squad mates to move into position in the center and draw out the Locust. While they do that, use the opportunity to move from cover to cover along the yard's left-hand side, advancing toward the Crimson Omen in the distance. This provides the perfect flanking opportunity for eliminating the Locust wave before it can do any harm.

Gather up the grenades and ammunition at the base of the stairs and ascend to the upper structure. There's no time for enjoying the ancient architecture right now though, as an Emergence Hole just opened at the yard's far right-hand corner! Let Dom and the others lure the enemies toward them while you flank to the left.

Make your way across the yard while moving from pillar to pillar, using the Lancer against each of the Locust. Should any of them get too close (or you get the opportunity to sneak up behind one), hold the B Button to saw them in half with the chainsaw bayonet.

COG TAG 04

Unlike the other COG Tags, one of Marcus' squad mates actually mentions this one's location. It's on the ground, just beyond the last short wall in the yard's center. Look to the right of the Crimson Omen.

At the rear of the yard, switch to grenades and lob one into the Emergence Hole in the corner. This hole leads directly underground to the massive network of Locust caverns—it must be sealed off before reinforcements arrive. Throwing a Frag Grenade down into it is the only way to accomplish this.

CLOSE THAT HOLE!

Emergence Holes (a.k.a. "grub holes") pose a major threat to Delta Squad and should be sealed off as quickly as possible. Most Emergence Holes continue to spew forth wave after wave of Locust Drones (and other assorted baddies) until it has been destroyed. Pressing the Y Button helps you locate each Emergence Hole as it appears, as does looking for the shimmering green glow that emanates from below. Additionally, most every Emergence Hole is marked on the maps in this guide, so use this information to your advantage.

With the Emergence Hole sealed, return toward Kim and the others and climb the stairs in the center of the yard. The others advance on the ground around the temple's side and lure out additional Grunts. By taking the upper walkway, Marcus gains a height advantage and gets the perfect angle to toss a grenade straight down into the lot of them. Descend from atop the ramped rubble pile and follow the others out onto the bridge, where Lieutenant Kim thinks he may have found Alpha Company.

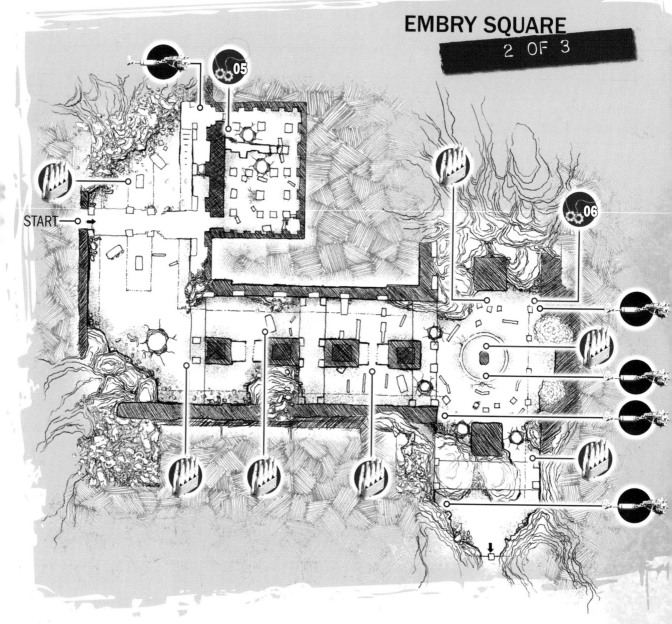

START

EMERGENCE HOLES

Kim opens the door to the inner yard and, just as he does, you hear an Emergence Hole ripping open to the left. Take cover behind the masonry to the left, and use the Lancer to rip apart any Drones that attempt to rush your squad. A second Emergence Hole opens at the other end of this area when you are in the second half of the room and the earthquake occurs. Clear out everyone from the first hole before you advance and trigger the second one. Cross the yard to the right and zigzag back to take out the next batch of Drones.

FISH IN A BARREL

Taking heat in Embry Square.

TAKE OUT THE TROIKA GUN EMPLACEMENT

There's little time to mourn, as a couple of Locust at a Troika mounted gun emplacement open fire on Delta Squad's position! Leave your allies safely behind cover, and Roadie Run around the uplifted asphalt near the Emergence Hole. This gets you safely to the other side of the pillars. Use the wall in the middle of the road for cover, and flank the two near the Troika. Lob a grenade at them through the opening to make the route safe for the others.

CONTINUE TO SEARCH FOR ALPHA SQUAD

Duck through the passage and mount the Troika by pressing the X Button. Quickly wheel around and open fire on the three Locust advancing toward your position. It takes a moment to rev up to speed, but the Troika can cut any enemy into pieces with just a couple rounds from its high-caliber shells.

COG TAG #05

Eliminate the Locust that emanate from the second Emergence Hole in this inner yard area. Then grab the COG Tag hidden in the weeds beyond it before you descend to the street.

Descend the steps to the street. Follow Kim beyond the bridge you crossed earlier to the corpses near the massive Emergence Hole. The COG Tags have been taken from the bodies. There's no way to tell if they are the remains of Alpha Squad or if they've been placed simply as bait. That answer comes soon enough...

Additional Locust have taken cover further down the road, near the plaza in the distance. Zigzag back to the right, through the second opening in the wall, and kill the Locust there. Then cut back through the third opening to move into a perfect close-range position to eradicate the remaining Grunts.

Kim, Dom, and Carmine move into position up ahead, amongst the empty wishes inside the plaza's waterless fountain. Meanwhile, you should quickly gather up the grenades lying around the area's periphery. One by one, four Emergence Holes open (see map) and groups of Locust Grunts pour out. Let the rest of the guys handle the Locust while you focus on closing those Emergence Holes! Use the maps and the Y Button to anticipate where the next Emergence Hole opens, and have a grenade ready for when it does. With some practice—and some good timing—you can successfully lob a grenade into the hole the moment it opens (watch for the asphalt to turn ashen), closing it before anything escapes.

COG TAG #06

Look to the area's far left corner, near the batch of grenades and ammunition box. This COG Tag lies on the ground. It's to the far left, opposite the fourth Emergence Hole.

HOUSE OF SOVEREIGNS

START

FORK IN THE ROAD

Delta Squad divides and conquers in Embry.

RIGHT PATH

CONTINUE TO SEARCH FOR ALPHA SQUAD

Taking the right-hand path pits Marcus and Carmine in the role of bait, allowing Dom and Kim to get into position to take out the Troika up ahead. Proceed up the ramp and around the corner, and quickly duck into the first hallway on the left to escape the Troika's line of fire. To help the others, shoot through the wooden boards in the wall to kill the Locust in the adjacent room. This allows Dom and Kim to take out the Locust manning the Troika via the boarded-up windows to the right.

Take control of the Troika, using it to chop down the pair of Locust approaching from the rear. With these last two defeated, Marcus is ready to rejoin Dom and Kim.

LEFT PATH

CONTINUE TO SEARCH FOR ALPHA SQUAD

The left path places Marcus and Carmine in slightly more immediate danger, as they have to cut their way through more Locust Drones on their way up the stairs initially. At the top of the stairs, they can enter the room to the left and take out the Gunner and Spotter by shooting them through the wooden boards. This gives Dom and Kim a chance to safely proceed through the hallway without getting shot to pieces. From here, continue through the bathrooms and out the door to regroup.

Three more Locust are stationed at the far end of the room ahead: two atop an elevated platform on the left, manning a Troika; and a Spotter in the room across from them to the right. Leave the rest of Delta Squad safely behind cover, and lead Marcus through the two rooms to the right and into cover behind the toppled tank. From there, lean to the right and take out the Spotter in the window above. This allows Marcus to flank those near the Troika. Kick open the door beneath the window, climb the stairs, and lob a Frag Grenade at the Gunner to silence the Troika.

The moment the Troika's Gunner is eliminated, an Emergence Hole opens up in this area's back corner. Man the Troika and kill the Locust as they spawn. When the Emergence Hole is sealed, a Drone kicks open the door that allows you to proceed. Exit through the door near the Troika to proceed toward the House of Sovereigns.

KNOCK KNOCK

Infiltrate the House of Sovereigns.

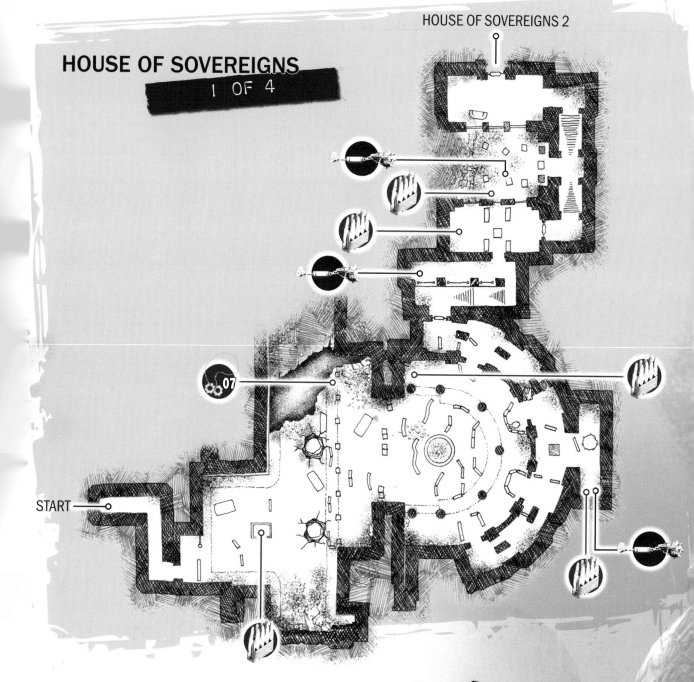

HOUSE OF SOVEREIGNS
1 OF 4

07

START

GAIN ENTRANCE TO THE HOUSE OF SOVEREIGNS

Proceed outside to the main plaza in front of the House of Sovereigns. There is a large number of Locust at the top of the stairs. They guard the semi-circular entrance area, but they don't appear until Marcus reaches the fountain. For now, take a moment to get your bearings and to collect the COG Tag to the left.

COG TAG #07

It's hard to miss the Crimson Omen on the side of the white van, but the COG Tag is a bit harder to spot. It's located on the steps to the left of the van, near the enormous crack in the street.

When you're ready to engage the Locust, approach the sandbags to the right of the fountain and take cover. The first wave of Locust Grunts emerges from the doors already opened, near the Troika. But Marcus should fix his sights on the right-hand door that has yet to open. A Grenadier soon bursts through the door, so be ready!

Once you eliminate the Grenadier, move into position near this door on the right and help Dom and the others by shooting a few of the Grunts nearing the fountain. Although the Troika is a concern, the Emergence Hole inside the main hallway is even more pressing. Use the available cover in the curving hall as you fight your way toward the left to close in on the hallway. Pick up some grenades from the bodies of the Grenadiers that emerge, and seal the hole before more arrive. By the time Marcus accomplishes this, the others likely have eliminated the Locust manning the Troika.

As you step back outside the entrance hall, you see that the battle isn't over yet. Two Emergence Holes open in the street, and a large army of Grunts and Grenadiers swarm toward Delta Squad's location. Man the Troika and cut them down as they approach.

The final few Locust appear from behind the remaining closed door. Turn and fire on them to neutralize the threat. Take a moment to collect the dropped ammunition and Frag Grenades from the corpses, and prepare to head inside the House of Sovereigns—Kim knows the code.

GNASHER AVAILABLE!

In addition to dropping Frag Grenades, Grenadiers also drop Gnasher guns and ammo. The Gnasher is a shotgun-style weapon with incredible short-range firepower. No sense holding onto both the Lancer and the Hammerburst; drop the latter in favor of the Gnasher!

SAVE THE ALPHA SQUAD SOLDIER

Your team might be down to three for the time being, but it won't be for long. The first thing you hear upon entering the House of Sovereigns is the unmistakable sound of one bad soldier getting his kill on in a distant room. Ascend the stairs to the balcony above to get a view of the action. From there, Marcus and the others can try to destroy the Grenadier engaged in a firefight with the soldier, but they can't prevent the deadly Frag Grenade that's lobbed at the soldier.

Wait for Lieutenant Kim to unlock the door to the right, and descend the stairs to rescue the soldier. Eliminate any remaining Drones or Grenadiers in the area, and press the X Button near the soldier to revive him. Augustus Cole (a.k.a. Cole Train) of Alpha Squad happily joins Marcus' group and even helps explain why radios are jammed. In short, it's because of the Seeders. Climb the stairs to the left and proceed through the doorway into the next hall.

HOUSE OF SOVEREIGNS
2 OF 4

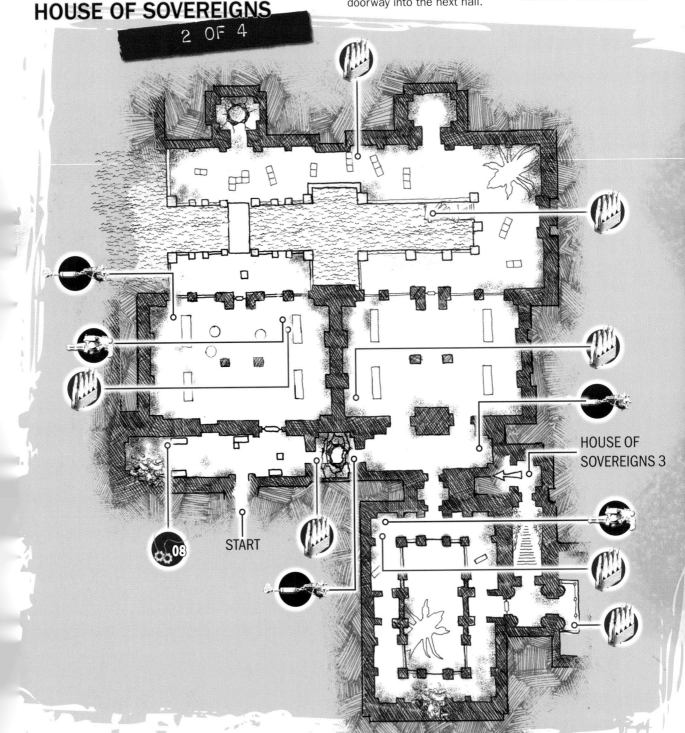

START

HOUSE OF
SOVEREIGNS 3

08

DESTROY ALL SEEDERS

The door that leads out of the hallway up ahead is welded shut and requires Delta Squad's trusty robot Jack to burn open. But don't expect to just sit around waiting for him to do his job. Nearly two dozen Wretches flood the room from both directions, trying to rip Marcus and the others to shreds. Wretches can run across the walls and ceiling, and they're more nimble than most every other Locust species, but they are very weak. It takes only one or two rounds from the Lancer to put down a Wretch, and a blast from the Gnasher positively blows one into bite-size morsels of gooey flesh.

Use the Lancer to take out the Wretches approaching from the far left end of the corridor. Then switch to the Gnasher to handle those on the right. They continue to crawl out of the massive Emergence Hole to the right of the sealed door until you kill the last of them—anticipate blasting roughly a dozen from the left, followed by an additional eight to ten from the right.

Step outside toward the canal and press the Y Button to focus in on the Seeder in the distance. Immediately break right before the bridge is lowered and hit the Seeder with the Hammer of Dawn. It's a lot easier to fight off the Drones if you no longer have to worry about the Nemacysts. One down, two to go! With the bridge lowered, throw a Frag Grenade into the Emergence Hole that's in the alcove beyond the bridge.

COG TAG #08

Enter the library and collect the **Hammer of Dawn** and ammunition from the floor to the right of the door (drop the Gnasher for the time being). The Hammer of Dawn is a special weapon that's useful for killing those enemies that are immune to traditional weaponry, such as the Seeders.

Cross through the second library room to the two-story room ahead. Ignore the Seeder on the lower floor for now and, instead, concentrate on fending off the first wave of Wretches and Nemacysts. When the coast is clear, use the Hammer of Dawn to blast the Seeder.

TIME TO MULTITASK

Don't concentrate so much on the Seeder that you neglect the Wretches and Nemacysts. Although your squadmates do a fairly good job protecting you from attack, the occasional foe does slip through. To prevent this, hit the Seeder with a short blast from the Hammer of Dawn and then quickly switch back to the Lancer and help eradicate any incoming threats. Repeat this tactic until the Seeder is destroyed.

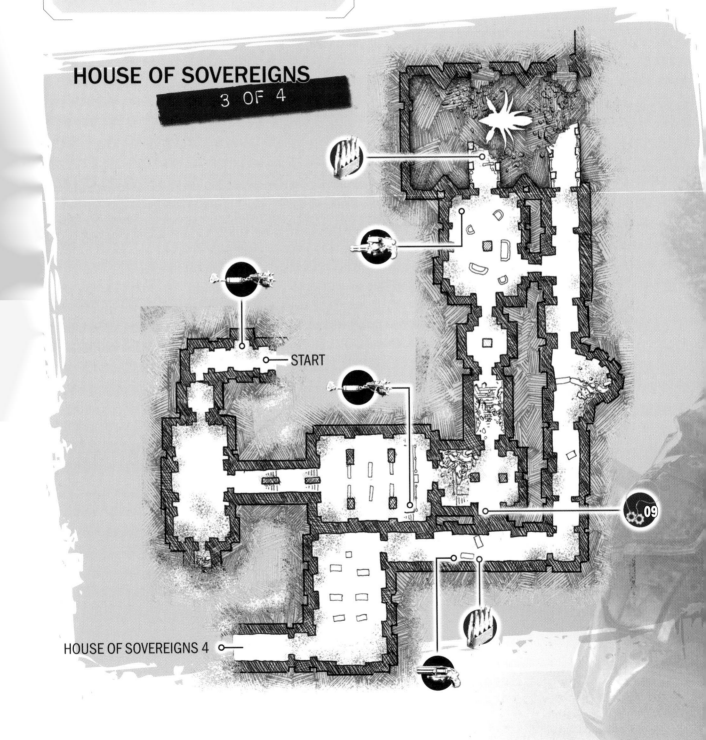

START

09

HOUSE OF SOVEREIGNS 4

Follow Lieutenant Kim to the door on the left side, and descend the stairs to the first floor. Kill the Wretches and proceed past the Seeder's corpse, into the sanctuary ahead. Take cover behind the sanctuary's pews and help the rest of Delta Squad wipeout the incoming Locust.

WRATH

A bloody reunion with Alpha Squad.

Eliminate the Drones in the room ahead, and step out onto the ruined walkway bridge in the upcoming courtyard. The third and final Seeder is just below. Help Kim and take out the Drones across the yard and on the bridge to the right, not to mention any Nemacysts that appear. Then switch to the Hammer of Dawn to take out the Seeder. As with the previous Seeder, don't focus on it for too long; alternate between targets, as the Nemacysts will surely end your mission prematurely if you don't.

SEARCH FOR ALPHA SQUAD

Lieutenant Kim calls Anya to let her know about the destruction of the Seeders. In the process, communication is made with the rest of Alpha Squad—they're outside and pinned down. They need your help, pronto!

Return to the previous room and use a Frag Grenade on the Locust cutting through the side door. Then head down the hall to the right. There is a **Boltok Pistol** up ahead, around the corner in the hall. This Locust-brand revolver packs an incredible amount of firepower in its tiny size, so don't underestimate it.

COG TAG #09

Exit the sanctuary, descend the stairs into the next room, and look behind the pillar to the right. It's hard to see, but the COG Tag is on the floor in the shadowy area on the side.

CAMPAIGN WALKTHROUGH

You can try out the Boltok Pistol immediately against the Drones in the room ahead. They take cover behind the desks, so fix your targeting sights just above the desk's surface and wait for them to pop up. A pair of Grenadiers isn't too far off, so don't let down your guard just yet!

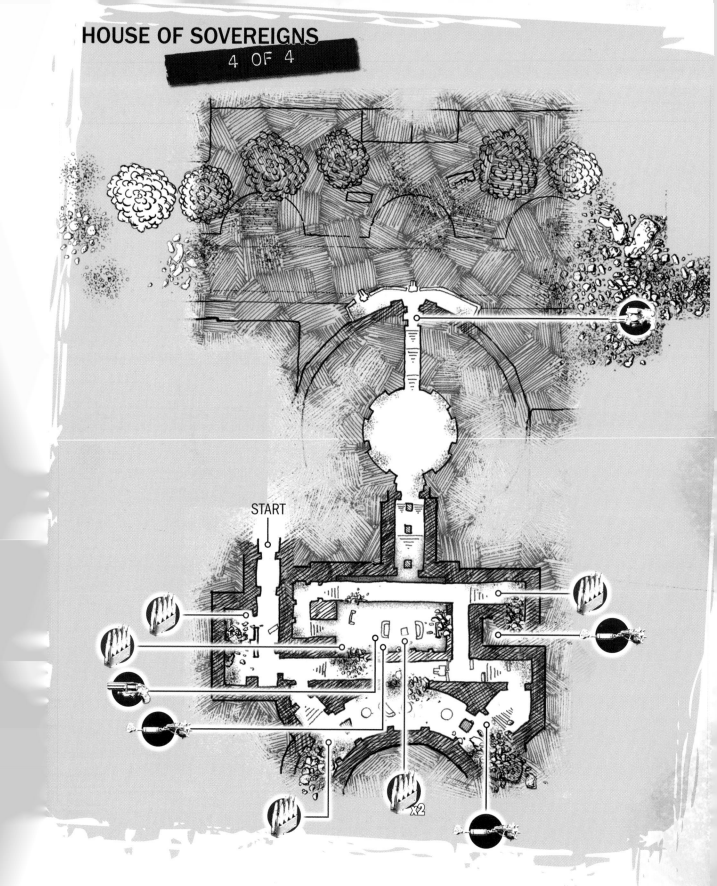

START

Grab the ammo from the room on the right and slowly approach the corner up ahead. A Drone has a Troika fixed on this end of the hallway and is just itching to lay some hurt on the first thing that peeks around the corner. Roadie Run toward the stairs and dive into the curving room on the right.

Fight past the Locust Drones and a small group of Wretches in this outer walkway to flank the Troika. Sneak up behind the Drone that operates it. There are few things more satisfying that revving up the Lancer's chainsaw bayonet behind an unsuspecting enemy. Additional Wretches pursue Delta Squad, but keep moving through the corridors and down the stairs.

The Locust inside the House of Sovereigns prepare a final ambush to keep Delta Squad from reaching the Troikas mounted on the balcony above the street. Stop on the landing above the final staircase, and ready a Frag Grenade for the Drones and Grenadiers that soon move into view below. Let them have it, then hurry down the stairs and to the left to flank the remaining Drones that usually seek cover behind the statue and furniture.

BEAT THE STUFFING OUT OF YA!

Not all cover is created equal. Many interior objects that provide cover are easily destroyed with enough firepower. The Lancer or Hammerburst can make quick work of sofas, desks, bookcases, crates, and other similar objects. Naturally, stronger weapons can be used the same way.

Climb the stairs to the balcony overlooking the street. A final Grenadier stands near the Troika, but the Troika can't swivel around to be a threat. Take him out!

SECURE THE LANDING ZONE FOR EVACUATION

There are two Troikas on the balcony. Marcus can use them to annihilate the remaining Locust forces on the ground below. Additionally, two unreachable Seeders spew forth a seemingly endless stream of Nemacysts in the far-off distance. Use the Troikas and the Lancer to eliminate this threat. Kim, Dom, and Cole certainly help but this is clearly Marcus' moment to shine behind the Troikas.

The key to surviving this battle is to avoid concentrating for too long on the Drones in the street below. They're not the main threat to Delta Squad—the Nemacysts are. Use the Troika to take down a couple Drones and then either back away from the Troika and use the Lancer to take out the Nemacysts or, if you're using the Troika in front of the stairs, blast the Nemacysts as they level off and enter the gun's line of fire. Don't let up until the Nemacysts stop coming and the last Drone is put down.

MOVABLE HAMMER

Another option is to grab the Hammer of Dawn at the top of the stairs and use it to chase the Drones between bursts of Nemacysts. Once the satellites triangulate the target location and the energy beam fires, you can eviscerate multiple enemies by adjusting the Hammer of Dawn's aim with the Right Thumbstick. Just don't forget about those Nemacysts!

CHINA SHOP

Berserker bait.

TOMB OF THE
UNKNOWNS

FIND ANOTHER WAY OUT

The Locust army's ambush was both unexpected and saddening. Not only are Delta and Alpha Companies unable to go home, but good men also have died. And now the only way out seems to be through the Tomb. On the positive side, at least your squad is still at maximum capacity thanks to the addition of Baird. But this is cold comfort considering the Berserker that's running loose in the Tomb.

COG TAG #10

Here is the one true instance in which you can collect a recently fallen soldier's COG Tag. Go around the corner, toward the spot where the Berserker killed the soldier at the beginning of the level. Look near the flames on the right.

VIDEO FOOTAGE
WATCH THE SHOWDOWN WITH THE BERSERKER.
bradygames.com/gearsofwar

BUY IT FIRST ON XBOX LIVE

START

LURE THE BERSERKER OUTSIDE

Your only hope against the Berserker is to lure her outside where the Hammer of Dawn can pound her. Berserkers are blind—which works to your advantage—but they have acute senses of hearing and smell.

Proceed through the Tomb toward the Berserker—Marcus runs into her in the hallway just beyond the first main room. Stand in the center of the hall and wait for her to charge, then dive to the side to avoid her. Use the Lancer to lure her away from Dom, who is at the rear of the hall, and slip through the door to the elongated room to the right. Use sporadic gunfire bursts to lure the Berserker out of the hallway and into the large room.

DON'T DIE ON ME, DOM!

There's a good chance that the Berserker will down Dom in the hallway where you run into her. If this happens, concentrate on luring the Berserker into the room to the right, just as if Dom hadn't been hit. Once she's in the other room, hurry back and revive Dom; he can't bleed out on his own, but he can get gibbed by the Berserker if she hits him again.

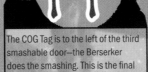

From here, it's a matter of using the Berserker's tremendous strength to knock down three heavy steel doors separating a sequence of rooms in the Tomb. Each of these doors are in the center of the far end of the wall. Rush forward to the door, turn around and shoot the Berserker to get her to rampage towards the door. Dive out of the way, lure her back into the room you're in, then slip through the door to the next room and repeat the process on the next door.

COG TAG #11

The COG Tag is to the left of the third smashable door—the Berserker does the smashing. This is the final door before you exit the Tomb to the courtyard.

KILL THE BERSERKER

COG TAG #12

Immediately after you lure the Berserker outside, go to the left along the curved portion of the semi-circular courtyard and look for the Crimson Omen. The COG Tag is on the ground just beyond it, directly against the main wall.

With the Berserker in the courtyard, switch to the Hammer of Dawn. Once you hit her with the Hammer of Dawn she glows red, indicating that she's vulnerable. At this point, any weapon will hurt her. Chances are, you'll have only about five or so minutes of satellite coverage, so don't waste much time (other than to get the COG Tag). Lead the Berserker toward an unbreakable wall or ledge so that she stuns herself slamming into it. Then put the Hammer of Dawn to work. It should take only two or three lengthy blasts to finish her off.

ACT 2: NIGHTFALL

BOOMER
These enormous members of the Locust Horde are outfitted with the Boomshot rocket-launcher weapon. They are very resilient but also very slow. Duck for cover when you hear them yell "Boom!"

SNIPER
Snipers are very similar to Drones, but they are equipped only with the Longshot rifle and are almost always out of Marcus' direct reach. Look for them in the windows of nearby buildings or on rooftops.

KRYLL
Despite their size, the Kryll are arguably the most fearsome creatures in all of Sera. There is no way to combat them with conventional weaponry, and they are so numerous, it would be a futile cause anyway. Stay out of the dark, or else.

ACT

NIGHTFALL

2

SITUATION
REPORT

If mankind should ever fall, it will likely be the vast extent of our collective hubris that does us in. Thinking Alpha and Delta Squad could repel the Locust Horde long enough to land a chopper at the House of Sovereigns is just the kind of conceit that gets good men killed—may those pilots and Lieutenant Kim rest in peace. And now, with hopes of an evacuation crushed, Marcus and his squad are instructed to take the resonator and hoof it to the distant Lethia Imulsion Factory—a destination they cannot reach before sunset. The team has been fighting the Locust Horde long enough to know that hitting the streets of Ephyra after dusk is certain suicide. If they're to survive, they'll have to swallow their pride and rely on the help of the Stranded.

13
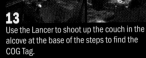
Use the Lancer to shoot up the couch in the alcove at the base of the steps to find the COG Tag.

14
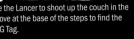
Exit the room with the collapsing catwalk, descend the stairs, and look behind the rubble in the alley.

15

Look behind the mailbox and newspaper box on the sidewalk before you pass through the gate to the settlement.

16
Look behind the mailbox and newspaper box on the sidewalk before you pass through the gate to the settlement.

16
This one is located in the shack near the propane tank, to the far left of the first Emergence Hole after you leave the camp.

17
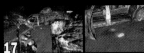
Use the spotlight to light up the area near the rusted car in order to reach the COG Tag without being killed by the Kryll.

18

Near the car with the propane tank in it, to the right of the doorway you exit. Shoot the tank to spread some light on the area, and quickly pick up the COG Tag before running down the street.

TICK TICK BOOM
Locust counterattack.

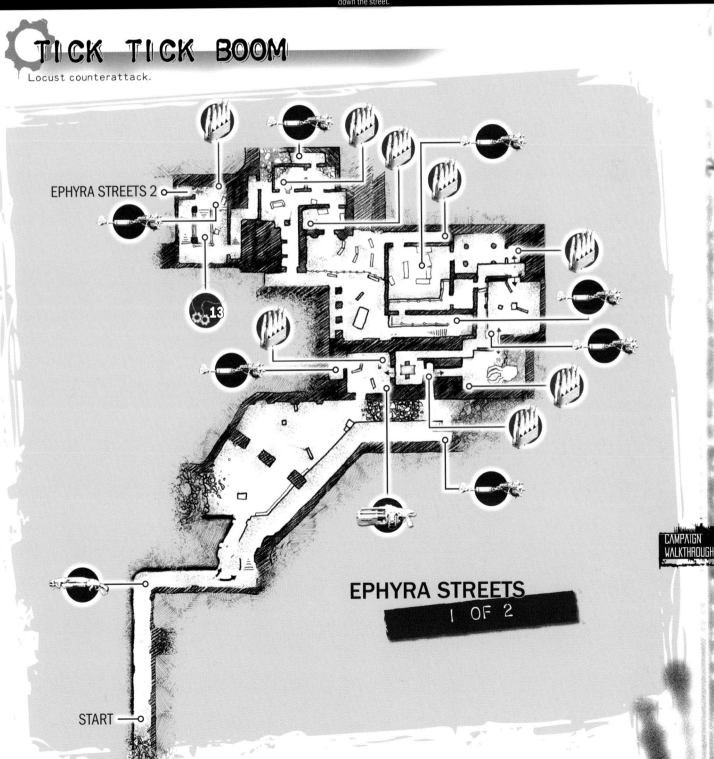

EPHYRA STREETS 2

13

EPHYRA STREETS

1 OF 2

START

FIND A MODE OF TRANSPORT

Whether he likes it or not, Marcus is stuck with Baird for the time being. Descend into the trench and follow it to the far end, where some extra Frag Grenades can be found—be sure to grab them! Exit the trench, ascend the stairs inside the building, and turn left.

This two-story room contains a pair of Boomers down below. If Marcus and Baird don't do something fast, those big fellows will unload on Gus and Dom. Switch to the Frag Grenades and take time to aim so that it bounces directly behind the two Boomers, who are unaware of your presence. Get it close enough, and that lone Frag Grenade will clear the path for the other guys.

Continue through the hall to the right and advance toward the Drone behind the toppled pillar up ahead. The twosome down below may need some extra firepower, so be sure to give a hand with the Lancer if necessary. Follow the path out onto the fire escape and descend to the street. Make sure to grab the Frag Grenade under the stairs near the couch, and *slowly* exit the alley with a Frag Grenade in hand.

Aim the Frag Grenade at an angle toward the barricade near the building's corner, and watch for the two Grenadiers to come into view. To drop the Grenadiers as quickly as possible, try to bounce the Frag Grenade up against the barricade (to stop it from sliding). Dom and Gus enter the area on the opposite side of the chainlink fence to the right. Use the Gnasher to take out the Grenadier approaching your position. Then turn to help the others by shooting through the fence with the Lancer.

Marcus and Baird are one short hallway away from rejoining the others, but there's a Troika at the far end. Give the "Cease Fire" command so that everyone takes cover, most notably Baird. This opens up an opportunity for Marcus to lob a Frag Grenade down the hall toward the Gunner—Roadie Run down the hall and duck into cover to get close. Should you be out of Frag Grenades, issue the "Attack" command to coerce Dom and Gus into ambushing the Gunner. Help them out by distracting the Gunner's attention from afar.

LEFT PATH: LOW ROUTE

FIND A MODE OF TRANSPORT

Gus and Dom take the trench and leave Baird and Marcus to look for another route. Cross through the open yard to the left and enter the rubble-strewn building beyond the pillars. Inside, a pair of Boomers emerges from the room to the right. Take cover behind the toppled pieces of concrete, and give the other guys (who are on a balcony above the Boomers) an opportunity to take out one of them. Use Frag Grenades and the Lancer to finish off the surviving Boomer as it comes through the door.

Make your way around the Corpser hole in the distance, and take cover in the courtyard near the statue. Dom and Gus help take out the Drones that appear, but be ready to fight back just in case the Drone makes its way under the balcony and out of the others' view.

Continue through the room with the empty shelving, and use the button near the door to exit into the alley outside. Throw several Frag Grenades over the chainlink fence on the left to kill the two Grenadiers marching toward Dom and Gus. With the Grenadiers put down, it's time to worry about Marcus and Dom. Take cover behind the stone blocks and sweep through the yard and into the building on the right, killing each Locust along the way.

The Gunner in the next room has Dom and Gus pinned down on the other side, but it quickly swivels the Troika in Marcus' direction if he's seen. Take cover as close to the Troika as possible, and give the "Attack" command to get Baird to rush the Spotter. This distracts the Gunner, thus giving Marcus a clear shot at him. Dom and Gus soon join up with Baird and Marcus.

After you clear the area, gather up the ammo and have Jack cut the door to the left of the Troika. Follow the path through the next building and into the next area. Dom knows one of the Stranded and thinks he can borrow a vehicle, so he'll lead the way to a camp.

COG TAG #13

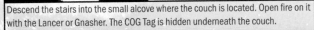

Descend the stairs into the small alcove where the couch is located. Open fire on it with the Lancer or Gnasher. The COG Tag is hidden underneath the couch.

EPHYRA STREETS
2 OF 2

FIND THE STRANDED'S SETTLEMENT

The fight outside the building comes fast and hard, and it doesn't let up until Marcus and his team eliminate multiple Drones, a Boomer, and even a pair of Snipers. Use Frag Grenades at the battle's start to reduce the immediate threat, then give the "Attack" command to the rest of Delta Squad. This is certain to eliminate the Boomer along with any Drones and Grenadiers that are still standing.

With the Boomer destroyed, give the "Cease Fire" command to have everyone duck for cover—there are two Snipers in the building down the road to the right. Try lobbing a Frag Grenade into the lower window, as the blast may well take out both Snipers. If not, use the Lancer to punish the upstairs Sniper when he looks to take his next shot.

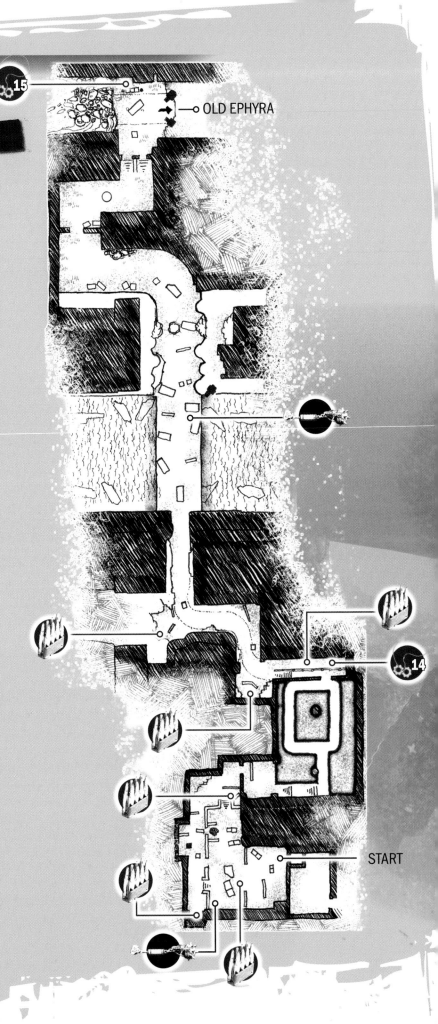

15

OLD EPHYRA

14

START

COG TAG #14

Descend the stairs outside the room with the circular catwalk, and enter the alley to the right. Look behind the small piece of rubble to find the COG Tag.

Climb the stairs in the factory ahead and follow the catwalk clockwise to the exit. Cut a path through the approaching Wretches to return to the street level outside. Load up on ammunition and fight your way past the next set of enemies to reach the bridge. You may want to pick up the Boomshot from the defeated Boomer along the way.

There's a Troika mounted on the far right side of the bridge, not to mention a seemingly never-ending supply of Drones, Wretches, and Grenadiers exiting an Emergence Hole in the distance. Marcus has to close the hole if his crew is to get any closer to the settlement.

Take cover behind the car in the center of the road, and repeatedly tap the X Button to push it across the bridge toward the Troika. This provides adequate cover while Marcus moves into position near the tipped-over van on the right. From there, he can easily toss a Frag Grenade up toward the Troika and take out the Gunner. With the Troika silenced, give the "Attack" command to the others so they can begin pushing back against the numerous Locust flooding across the bridge.

Take your time and slowly make your way from cover to cover toward the Emergence Hole. Don't try to make a hero run and blow it up without adequate protection from the others, else you'll never make it back. Pay extra attention to the Wretches in this area, as it's easy to get sidetracked by the Grenadiers and forget the speedy little guys with the razor-sharp claws. This fight isn't easy, but the good news is that there's not a single other Locust between here and the gatekeeper at the Stranded's settlement.

COG TAG #15

The COG Tag is behind the mailbox and newspaper dispensers on the sidewalk, to the left of the gate outside the Stranded's settlement (as viewed while you face the gate).

OLD EPHYRA

1 OF 4

Dom takes over for Marcus at the settlement; after all, Dom is the one they know in these parts. Most of the Strandeds hurry inside and shutter the windows of their tin-can homes at the sight of the COGs, but not Franklin. Dom finds him in his usual spot, hawking his typical wares, and he begrudgingly agrees to fork over the keys to his ride. But there's a catch: Baird and Gus have to stay behind as collateral. That, and the fact that the Junker is all the way across town at Aspho Gas Station.

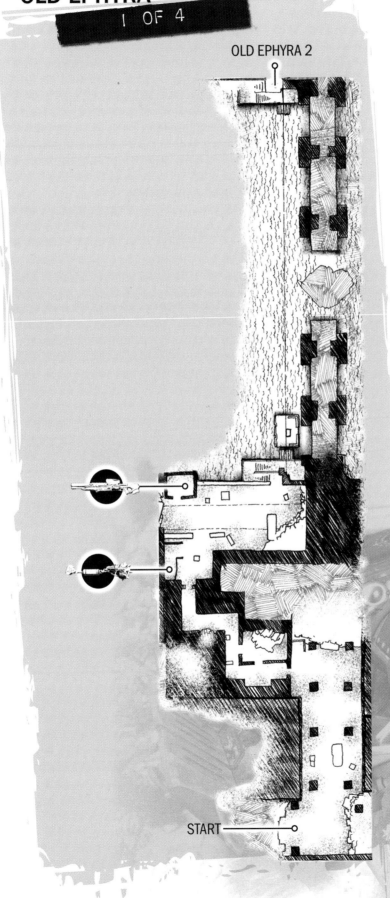

OLD EPHYRA 2

START

LETHAL DUSK

Stay in the light or be consumed.

CROSS THE RIVER TO CHECKPOINT I

Exit the settlement through the ruined building to the left of the rubble pile, and have your guns at the ready when you exit the other side. Several Drones and a Sniper defend the ferry near the river, and they mean business. Shoot the propane tank to detonate it. This helps illuminate the area and inflicts severe damage to anybody caught near the explosion. If the propane tank explosion doesn't eliminate the Sniper in the shack across the street, lob a Frag Grenade into it. Either way, make sure you kill him and grab the **Longshot** he drops.

YOU CAN BET ON THIS LONGSHOT!

The Longshot is a high-caliber sniper rifle with tremendous range and great optics. Shoulder the weapon and use the L and R Triggers to aim and fire as any other weapon. The big benefit to using the Longshot is that you can click the Right Thumbstick to zoom in on distant enemies. This makes it possible to strike with a perfectly-aimed headshot from hundreds of yards away.

Dom leads the way to the ferry. Board the ferry and get started cranking across the river as soon as Dom is aboard.

The ferry is connected to an overhead cable and is essentially hand-winched along the cable by turning the large wheel in the center of the platform. Dom uses his Gnasher and Lancer to defend the two of you from attacks as best he can, but watch Marcus' status and give Dom a hand if he starts to take too much damage. For the most part, Marcus can focus on turning the big wheel (press the A Button) until they reach the far bank.

CAMPAIGN WALKTHROUGH

OLD EPHYRA
2 OF 4

START

BEWARE THE KRYLL

The setting sun is not a romantic sight in Old Ephyra.
Here, it means one thing: the Kryll are out and they're
hungry! Stay in the light from here on, else you'll be
swarmed by the carnivorous Kryll. Listen for the sound
of their pre-feast screeching, as it's your only warning
that they're about to attack. You'll have no more than a
second or so to dive back into a well-lit area to avoid
getting devoured.

The guys at Checkpoint 1 are just up ahead. Climb the steps
to the main road and follow the light to the shacks on the
right. They don't look like much, but they contain a collection
of ammo and guns the likes of which Marcus hasn't seen
since his days in the Pendulum Wars. Load up, soldier!

GET TO CHECKPOINT 2

Cut through the well-lit and equally well-appointed house outside the Stranded camp. Rush for cover behind the burned-out cars in the street. An Emergence Hole has opened in the distance, and a crew of Grenadiers is heading your way. Take aim on the propane tank to the right of the car and the one in the middle of the street to give protection from the Kryll. Flank around the cars' right side and kill the first wave of Grenadiers. Then toss a Frag Grenade into the Emergence Hole. Alternatively, you can shoot out the lights to seal the Emergence Hole with Kryll. A Grenadier bursts out the door before the first pushcar.

COG TAG #16

The road turns to the right, but first shoot the propane tank off to the left, near the corrugated shack. There is a COG Tag located inside this shack, but you have to see the light in order to get it.

FUEL'S GOLD

The white propane tanks scattered throughout the streets of Old Ephyra are of the standard backyard barbecue variety, but here they represent the difference between life and death. Or, more appropriately, *light* and death. Shoot the tanks with the Lancer to detonate them. After the initial explosion, they burn at a controlled rate for several minutes, offering Marcus a chance to do what he needs to do. Some of the propane tanks are partially hidden by debris—just shoot it off from afar. Lastly, you can see the location of each propane tank on the maps in this guide (the small triangles).

Move into position behind the car in the middle of the road, and use the Longshot to snipe the Gunner and Spotter near the Troika at the street's far end. Marcus and Dom can then zigzag down the street, from propane tank to propane tank, to reach the entrance to the building on the left.

Cut through the building's lower floor to bypass the darkened area outside, and hop out the window to get the Frag Grenades near the Troika. From there, reenter the building, climb the stairs, and proceed out the other side.

DARK ENOUGH FOR YOU?

Looking to unleash a particularly nasty experience on the Locust Horde? If so, keep an eye out for enemies positioned near fluorescent overhead lights. Shooting these lights darkens their areas, instantly exposing them to a Kryll attack. This conserves ammo *and* it's fun to watch!

Another Emergence Hole has opened in the distance. This time, Marcus needn't seal it off head-on. Leave Dom to distract the Grenadiers and Drones from the front while Marcus flanks through the area to the left. Cut through the few Wretches that appear, and move all the way to the far end where there is a clear view of the Emergence Hole. Close the hole and then take out the remaining Locust from behind.

CAMPAIGN WALKTHROUGH

Cut through the ruins to the next street. Slip behind the nearby car remains to take cover from the Troika in the distance. Press the X Button repeatedly to push the car along the street to the barricade. From there, Marcus can snipe the Spotter in the upper right window (or shoot out the lights in that room), as well as the Drone in the building to the left of the Troika. Roll toward the barricade in front of the Troika and lob a Frag Grenade at the Gunner.

Anya wants Marcus and Dom to take the alley near the Troika, but it's pitch black. Before taking your chances with the Kryll (the Kryll always win, by the way), run through the hallway in the building near the Troika. You'll reach a hole in the wall. From there, Marcus can blast the propane tank behind the alley's dumpster to illuminate the pathway. Double back around the front and proceed according to Anya's instruction.

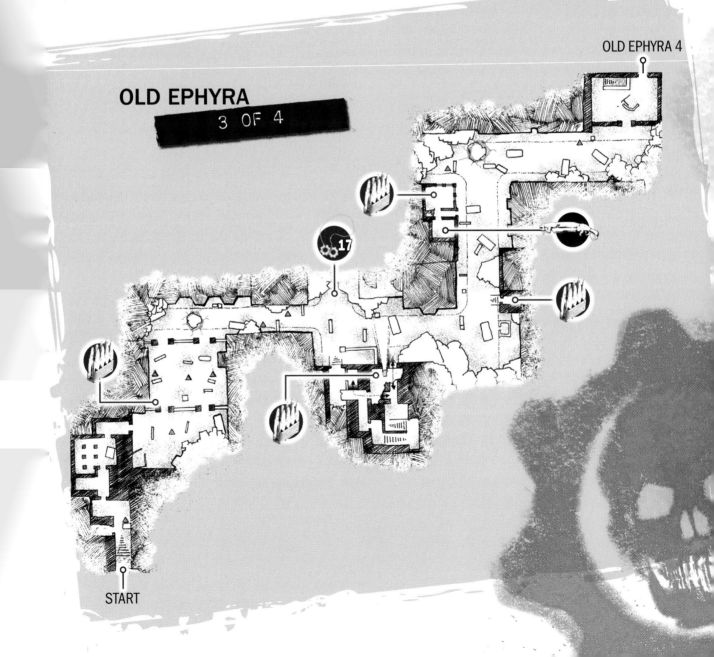

OLD EPHYRA 4

OLD EPHYRA
3 OF 4

17

START

GET TO CHECKPOINT 2

Proceed through the building beyond the alley and out into the courtyard on the other side. Slide in behind the barricade in front of the door and, together with Dom, take out the pair of Drones across the yard.

There are plenty of obstacles in the area between Delta One and the Emergence Hole, but there's also plenty of darkness. Using the Lancer, break apart the furniture to get a clear shot at the propane tanks in the yard's center before you push toward the Emergence Hole. Cross back to the left to circle in from behind the Emergence Hole, and drop a Frag Grenade into it. Help Dom clear out any surviving Grenadiers and Drones.

OUT OF FRAG GRENADES?

Even if you run out of Frag Grenades and there are no Grenadier corpses to loot, there's still a way to stem the seemingly endless stream of Locust emerging from the hole. Move in close to the Emergence Hole and kill all nearby Locust. Maintain your position near the Emergence Hole and continue to kill everything that comes out of it or near it. The Locust still lurking underground will realize that you're not one to be reckoned with, and they will stop using that particular hole.

Shoot the propane tanks on the sloping road to light the way toward the darkened street up ahead. In this area, Marcus must leave Dom behind and man the spotlight to help Dom safely work his way down the street. Issue the "Cease Fire" command to make Dom take cover and stay behind.

Enter the building on the right and follow the route to the platform on the third floor; that's where the spotlight is.

Grab hold of the spotlight and shine it on Dom. While he fights his way down the street, follow his movements with the spotlight to keep him safe from the Kryll. Once he reaches the other end of the road, he runs inside and powers up the lanterns strung across the street between the buildings.

COG TAG #17

Use the spotlight to illuminate the COG Tag in the darkened area to the far left, near the rusted car. Leave the spotlight positioned there and return to the street to collect it. Do this after you guide Dom to the power switch to avoid making a second trip up to the spotlight.

Meet up with Dom at the far end of the street and proceed together around the corner to the left. Leave Dom to distract the Locust coming out of the Emergence Hole in the distance while you flank them through the buildings on the left. Detonate the propane tank just outside the window in the far building, and leap out onto the street to seal the hole (or to kill the last Locust). Checkpoint 2 is just up ahead.

DARK LABYRINTH

Light your way to salvation.

OLD EPHYRA
4 OF 4

18

START

GET THROUGH THE RUINED HOUSE

The house is dark and contains a dozen or so Wretches, but it's primarily an easy jaunt from one side to the other. Keep to the lit areas, avoid the darkened hallways, and snake your way through the house to reach the street on the other side. Marcus has to destroy some furniture to get through it, but there's nothing that the Lancer's chainsaw bayonet can't handle. Chap's Gas Station isn't much further.

GET TO THE GAS STATION

The area outside the ruined house is incredibly dark. Fortunately, there's a propane tank in the back seat of the distant burned-out car. Shoot the tank and rush toward the car before the Kryll come.

COG TAG #18

This COG Tag is located near the car with the propane tank in it, to the right of the doorway you exit. Shoot the tank to spread some light on the area, and quickly pick up the COG Tag before running down the street.

There's no light between this end of the road and the gas station down the hill, but that doesn't mean you can't proceed. The explosion from the propane tank sets the car rolling down the hill toward Chap's Gas Station. Hold the A Button to Roadie Run after it—keep close to it, else the Kryll will be sure to get you!

BOOMSHOT

Grab the Boomshot that the Boomer drops at the gas station. It makes the Emergence Holes at Alamo very easy to close and it conserves Frag Grenades for later. A good strategy is to swap out the Gnasher for the Boomshot and hang on to the Longshot.

POWDER KEG

Shootout at Aspho Gas Station.

FUEL THE JUNKER AND ESCAPE.

Chap knew you were coming but figured that if Dom and Marcus want to borrow the Junker so bad, then they should be the ones to refuel it. Head over to the tanks on the side of the gas station and crank the valve to refuel it. Then enter gas station to collect the ammo and weaponry Chap has so graciously offered.

While you're inside the gas station, the Locust Horde descends en masse on your location, and a large-scale battle breaks out. Dom and Chap exit the gas station to take on the first wave descending from the staircase across the street. As Marcus, you should stay inside the gas station and use the Longshot to snipe this first wave of enemies. Several Wretches attack after a minute or so, so be ready to cave in their skulls with the butt of the rifle.

Dom announces the presence of a Boomer. This big fellow lumbers out of the garage behind the Junker. Stay within the gas station office and continue to use the Longshot until the Boomer is dropped. If left to his own devices, he gradually makes his way toward Marcus' position, but it's best to kill him quickly. Besides, the last thing ol' man Chap wants is a Boomshot going off near his fuel tanks!

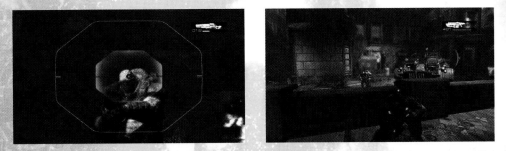

WATCH THE TANKS!

You can't continue fueling the Junker if you blow up the fuel tanks. Although Chap ceaselessly remind Marcus and Dom about the tanks, you don't have to worry about blowing up the place (and failing this mission) so long as you avoid shooting the propane tank near the gas pumps outside the office. Also, refrain from using Frag Grenades or firing the Boomshot (if applicable) anywhere near the gas pumps. Instead, stick with the Longshot and Lancer and you'll be all right.

CAMPAIGN WALKTHROUGH

Once the Boomer is eliminated, exit the office and take cover near the wall in the center of the street—just be sure to stay in the light. From there, Marcus can snipe the few remaining Drones. Afterward, Dom disconnects the fueling hose and the three men make their escape in the Junker.

BURNT RUBBER
Burn Kryll...while burning rubber.

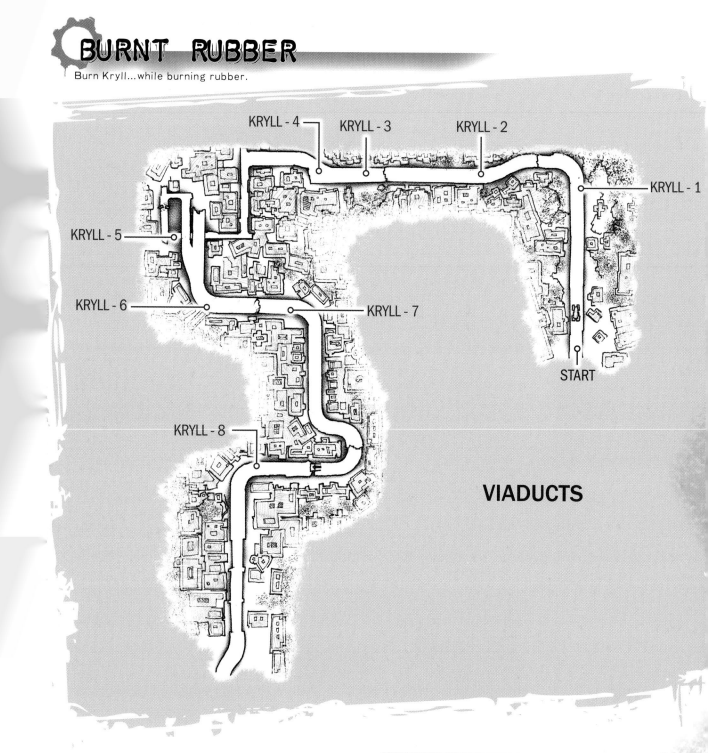

KRYLL - 4 KRYLL - 3 KRYLL - 2

KRYLL - 1

KRYLL - 5

KRYLL - 6 KRYLL - 7

START

KRYLL - 8

VIADUCTS

FUEL THE JUNKER AND ESCAPE

The Junker may look tough, but it offers little protection from the Kryll. The one hope Marcus and the others have of surviving the trip back to the encampment is to use the Junker's UV Turret to fend off the attacking Kryll swarms. The UV Turret instantly burns straight through the Kryll on contact, making it a formidable weapon against them.

OPERATING THE JUNKER

Despite its imposing appearance, the Junker can power only the engine or the UV Turret, but not both simultaneously. Whenever you spot the Kryll, you have to press the X Button to shut off the engine and direct power to the UV Turret. Pressing the X Button again shifts power back to the drive motors and gets the Junker rolling. You control the UV Turret just like the other weapons in *Gears of War*, except that its firing duration is rather short. When it comes time to drive the Junker, use the L and R Triggers for brake/reverse and accelerate, respectively.

Drive the Junker along the elevated highway toward the bend to the left. As you approach the curve, Chap spots the first two swarms of Kryll. Each time he spots Kryll, he lets out a warning and tries to announce their location relative to the direction the Junker is facing (e.g., 12 o'clock, 6 o'clock, etc.). Quickly switch to the UV Turret and blast the Kryll before they get too close. The UV Turret can be fired only for about two seconds at a time, so aim carefully!

The highway running between the gas station and the Stranded camp has definitely seen better days. The Viaducts are falling to pieces and there are burned-out cars and debris everywhere. Fortunately, the Junker's huge tires and battering ram front end make it the perfect vehicle for jumping off the highway's uplifted sections and for plowing through the debris. The route to the camp is straightforward, with the only sudden direction change coming when Chap instructs Marcus to exit the highway, loop through a few city blocks, and return to the elevated roadway a short distance ahead.

Despite the straightforward navigation, this is still a challenging mission, as the Kryll are as unrelenting at feeding time as any species known to man. Each of the swarm locations are marked on the accompanying map. Use the map in conjunction with the following table to better anticipate the direction and quantity of Kryll you'll encounter.

Location	No. of Swarms	Direction Relative to Junker
1	2	Both swarms at 12 o'clock
2	3	12 o'clock, 9 o'clock, then 6 o'clock
3	4	12 o'clock, 10 o'clock, then two swarms at 6 o'clock
4	1	11 o'clock
5	1	9 o'clock
6	4	Two swarms at 11 o'clock, then two swarms at 6 o'clock
7	2	Two swarms at 7 o'clock
8	3	Three swarms at 2 o'clock

SOLITARY KRYLL

With the UV Turret, Kryll are pretty easy to kill from a distance, but they can be downright pesky when one gets good and close. Should a single Kryll or two manage to reach the Junker's passenger compartment and evade your best efforts with the UV Turret, simply hit the X Button to shift power to the engines and drive away from it. Get a bit of distance on it, then switch control back to the UV Turret and turn to zap it.

LAST STAND

Fight alongside the Stranded.

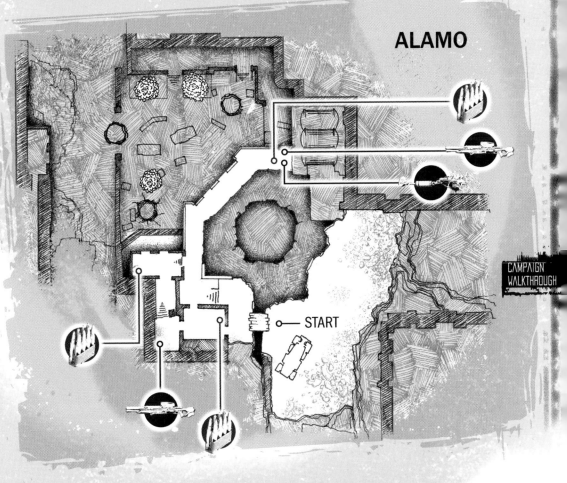

ALAMO

START

REPEL THE LOCUST ATTACK

Marcus and Dom get to the camp just in time to help Baird and thrashball all-star Gus "Cole" Train. Cross the wooden bridge on the left, leap through the window, and make your way toward Baird's position near the flaming toilet. This is a great place from which to close the Emergence Hole that opens. Use the Longshot to finish off any Drones still on the ground, and then get ready for the Snipers that come!

Head out onto the walkway near Dom and the Stranded, and take aim on the loose slab of concrete above the Snipers in the building to the left. Use the Lancer to loosen the concrete slab so it falls and crushes the Snipers below.

RANDOM ORDER

The second and third Emergence Holes, as well as the window Snipers and the roof gaspipe enemies, all appear in random order. Take that into account as you read the next several paragraphs of strategy

A second Emergence Hole opens in the distance. Exit the building onto the wooden walkway, and rush over to close the hole. While you're on that side of the platform, aim the Troika at the metal pipe above the enemies on the nearby building's second floor. Shoot the pipe to create a gas leak, and then continue shooting the pipe to spark an explosion. Rush back to the left to close the third Emergence Hole that opens, and quickly return to the Troika.

VIDEO FOOTAGE
WATCH THE EMERGENCE HOLES GET SHUT DOWN.
bradygames.com/gearsofwar

BUY IT FIRST ON XBOX LIVE

The Locust are set to kick the battle into overdrive when you close the third Emergence Hole, and a Boomer leads the charge. Use the Troika to gun down the Boomer, and then spray the Troika's high-caliber bullets across the building façade to the right. Continue firing at the many Drones and Grenadiers hiding inside the building's ground floor. Some may be difficult to hit with the Troika, so consider switching to Frag Grenades or the Lancer.

Surprisingly, the Locust have one final ambush left in them. A fourth and utterly massive Emergence Hole opens between the walkway and the Junker. Unlike other Emergence Holes, this one is so big that the four Boomers that appear within it can't even climb out. Instead, they stay within the sinkhole-like depression and open fire with their Boomshots.

The gigantic tremor resulting from this fourth Emergence Hole rattles one of the large fuel tanks off its rack. You can probably guess what comes next...

Although it's entirely possible to eliminate the four Boomers with the Lancer, Longshot, and Frag Grenades, it's much more fun to shoot the large fuel tank until it starts to leak fuel. Once you get the fuel flowing, shoot the small collection of propane tanks on the ground beneath the larger tank. This sets off an explosion of such magnitude that you might actually feel sorry for the Boomers caught in the blast.

The Locust invasion has been defeated, and Marcus and the others have more than earned the use of the Junker. It's time to head to the Imulsion factory.

ACT 3: BELLY OF THE BEAST

FIRST ENCOUNTERS

DARK WRETCH
Dark Wretches are similar to normal Wretches but they are black, are more aggressive, and explode when killed.

CORPSER
This monstrous creature resembles a hermit crab, except that it's the size of a house! Its mighty claws can deliver death with a single jab.

THERON GUARD
Theron Guards are faster, smarter, and stronger than standard Drones. These traits, combined with their possession of the Torquebow make them a fearsome foe.

ACT 3

BELLY OF THE BEAST

SITUATION REPORT

This isn't the first time a special COG unit has been dispatched with the goal of deploying a resonator—like device in the Imulsion mines. Unfortunately, that previous team was unmercifully slaughtered by the Locust Horde and direct access to the mine has been sealed off ever since. No, this time things are going to be much different. Not only must Delta Squad search for an alternate entrance through the Lethia Imulsion Facility, but they must be sure to get in and get out before sunrise. After all, with so few humans left to feed upon, the Kryll may still be hungry when they return.

19
At the far end of the narrow dock outside the Imulsion Facility.

21
Beside the stairs in the cart control room, near the mine carts.

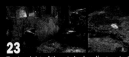

23
To the right of the stairs leading up to the small building beyond the bloody river.

20
In the far right corner of the room with the collapsing wooden floorboards.

22
In the first section of the mines, follow the path to the Crimson Omen straight ahead.

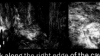

24
Walk along the right edge of the cave near the massive Imulsion pool to find the COG Tag on the narrow ledge.

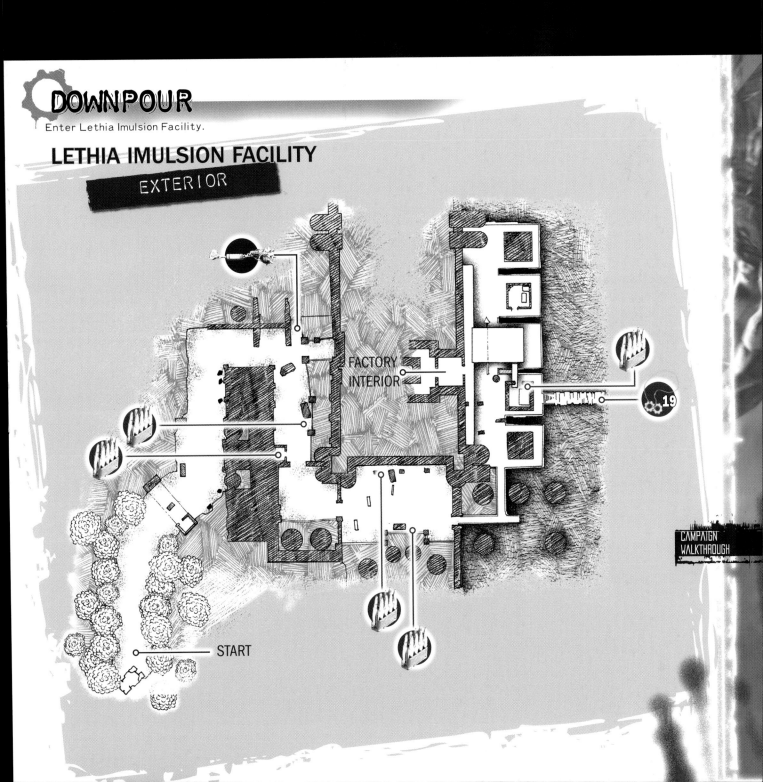

DOWNPOUR
Enter Lethia Imulsion Facility.

LETHIA IMULSION FACILITY
EXTERIOR

FACTORY INTERIOR

19

START

CAMPAIGN WALKTHROUGH

SCOUT THE FACTORY ENTRANCE

If the Junker had to break down, it couldn't have happened in a better spot. It might be dark and rainy, but the factory is just a short jaunt from here. Follow the dirt road to the factory entrance—the walk provides Delta Squad with a nice preview of the "wildlife" they'll encounter later on.

As can be expected in times like this, the main entrance to the facility has been locked and the doors are far too thick for Jack to rip open. Marcus decides the team should split up. He and Dom will look for an entrance near the docks, while Baird and Cole can look elsewhere.

FIND AN ENTRANCE TO THE FACTORY

Follow Dom down the path to the right, toward the large storage tanks near the docks. There's plenty of ammo to gather along the way, so be sure to grab it.

The Dark Wretches the team has seen scampering about the factory are finally ready to attack. Use the Lancer and shoot from the hip as you back away from them. If any get up onto Marcus, shoot to kill then quickly somersault away to avoid their post-mortem detonations. The first wave contains roughly eight Dark Wretches. Replenish your ammo and then approach the narrow walkway near the fluorescent light to lure out the second wave. Wipe out this last half-dozen or so Dark Wretches and continue toward the waterfront.

COG TAG #19

Go behind the building with the elevator in it, and walk out onto the narrow wooden dock. Run to the far end of the dock to find this hidden COG Tag.

The second brick building on the right side contains an elevator but the power is currently off. Anya believes there might be an external generator nearby. Naturally, Anya is correct. Enter the third building on the right and press the green-lit button to turn on the generator. Return to the elevator, ride it up to the tin rooftop, and climb through the window to enter the facility.

EVOLUTION

Keep your distance from Dark Wretches.

FACTORY INTERIOR 1B

LETHIA IMULSION FACTORY INTERIOR

1 OF 4

START

FIND THE CART CONTROL ROOM

Marcus and Dom enter the factory through an upper window. They need to find the cart control room in order for Anya to help them reach the mine. To do so, they have to navigate a long-abandoned factory with faulty electricity and a disturbing infestation of Dark Wretches.

DON'T FEAR THE SILENCE

Unlike the streets of Ephyra, the Lethia Imulsion Facility is relatively vacant of gun-toting enemies. Much of the journey to the cart control room takes place in bone-chilling isolation. Sure, Marcus and Dom will fend off dozens of Dark Wretches but their *imaginations* might get the best of them. This area is not for those afraid of things that go bump in the night.

CAMPAIGN
WALKTHROUGH

7

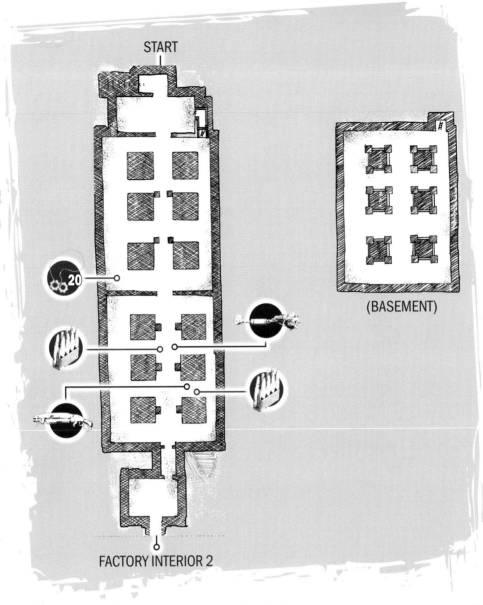

START

(BASEMENT)

20

FACTORY INTERIOR 2

The Stranded doesn't know the factory as well as he thinks he does. The poor guy walks out onto a crumbling wooden floor and falls into a pit of Dark Wretches in the basement. The wooden floor obviously has some structural weaknesses—the pattern of floorboards that collapse versus those that hold is random. Here's an easy solution: take one step forward; if you hear a creak, step back before the boards fall. Continue testing in this method as you go. The good news is that falling into the watery room below doesn't spell instant doom. If you fall, simply sprint back toward the direction you came and climb the ladder in the right corner. The Dark Wretches attack, but it's not that difficult to hold them off as you flee to the ladder.

Baird and Cole work on getting the lights turned on during their stroll through the basement (and later the sewers). While they do that, lead Marcus and Dom down the hall on the left and across the metal catwalk. Proceed to a room of unimaginable carnage. The door on the room's right side is locked and can't be opened without a security code, so head through the door to the left.

Turns out a Stranded has been holed up inside the factory awaiting rescue. He thinks Marcus is the savior he's been praying would come, and he's willing to unlock the other door and

lead the way to the cart control room. Follow him through the next several rooms and out into the lengthy processing room. Follow the Stranded around the perimeter walkway and down the stairs to the lower level.

LIMITED MOVEMENT AND NO GUNS

Marcus takes it nice and slow crossing this room so, no, you cannot somersault to safety when you hear the floor start to give way. Nor can you use the Lancer to shoot the flooring to see which boards stay and which break away. There's a very simple reason for this: even the flooring that can support his weight won't hold up to the stress of gunfire or acrobatics.

Although crossing the room does have a touch of trial-and-error to it, you can reduce the chance of falling by walking atop the metal support beams where the various floorboards come together. Some sections lack a support beam—walking on these boards is not a good idea. Either way, make your way over to solid ground, gather up the available ammo and Frag Grenades, and continue past the turbines to the next section.

COG TAG #20

This COG Tag is in the far right corner of the collapsing wooden floorboard room. From the starting point, go to the right and then hug the generators as you cross the room. Once you're near the COG Tag, walk across the metal beam to get it.

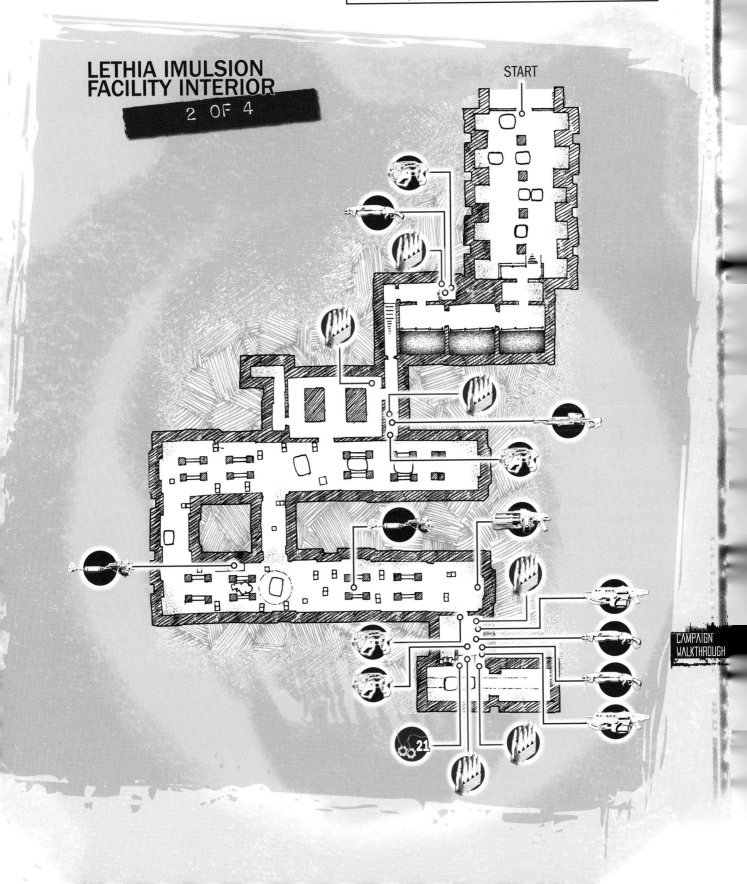

LETHIA IMULSION FACILITY INTERIOR
2 OF 4

START

21

FIND THE CART CONTROL ROOM

In the mine cart storage area up ahead, more than a dozen Dark Wretches attack Marcus and Dom. Make sure the Lancer is fully loaded and that there is plenty of room for evasive maneuvers on all sides. Rush forward toward the Dark Wretches as you shoot, then quickly reverse direction, backpedaling away from their explosions. Unlike dealing with other enemies, avoid locking into a cover position when you fight the Dark Wretches. Instead, keep moving and fire from the hip. Dom does a fine job helping to drop the Dark Wretches, but don't even think of lowering that rifle until the silence returns.

Continue through the next several rooms to a small office with a sealed door on either end. Turn the primer valve on the wall in the room's center to open the doors. Gather up the ammo and weapons in the closet, and then head down the stairs. Baird and Cole are in the room up ahead.

Turn the valve on the left wall (Cole raises the bars covering it from the other room) to raise the door, and enter the large processing room ahead. Unlike the previous rooms, this one contains more than just Dark Wretches; there are also a couple of Drones and Grenadiers. Good thing the whole team is back together again!

Enter the room and retreat to the left to put some distance between Marcus and the Drones at the far end. The rest of the team snuffs out most of the Dark Wretches that appear. While they handle those, use the Longshot to snipe any of the gun-toting Locust that show themselves. Alternate back and forth between the Longshot and the Lancer for the inevitable Dark Wretch that makes it through the front lines.

When the Dark Wretch invasion starts to subside, issue the "Attack" command to have the boys head out and hunt down the other remaining Locust. Round the corner to the right and advance slowly toward the locked door at the other end—this is the door to the cart control room. Marcus calls for Jack to rip open the door, but the second he does a Boomer and a Grenadier begin to descend on the nearby lift. Take cover behind the blocks and throw a Frag Grenade over the gate to greet them. Although Marcus can grab the Boomshot from the Boomer's remains, we recommend holding onto the Longshot for the time being.

Enter the cart control room and push the button on the control panel to the right to open the gates. It's time to go for a ride!

COG TAG #21

Descend the stairs to the row of mine carts and turn around. There is a COG Tag in the small gap between the stairs and the wall to the left.

COALITION CARGO

Mechanized death ride.

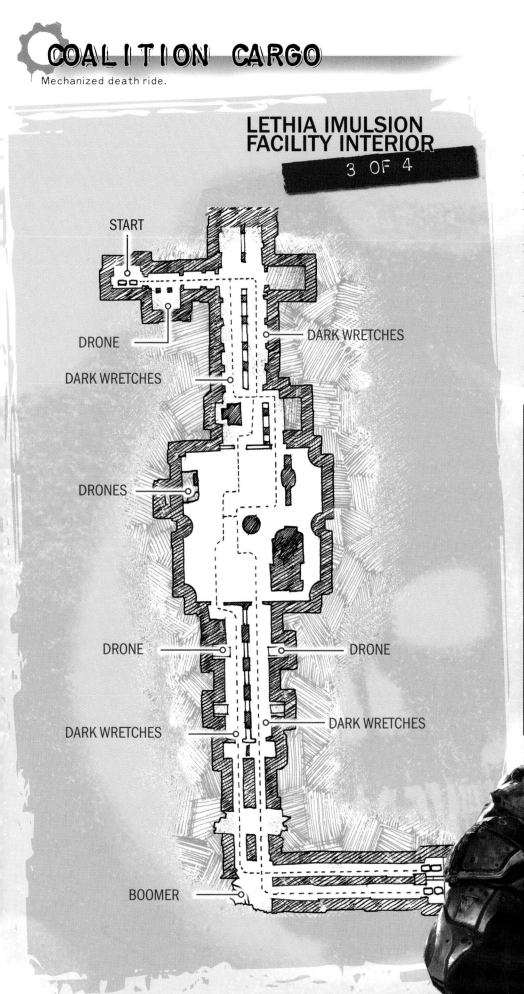

START

DRONE

DARK WRETCHES

DARK WRETCHES

DRONES

DRONE

DRONE

DARK WRETCHES

DARK WRETCHES

BOOMER

RIDE THE CARTS TO THE CORE ROOM

The ride to the core room takes place on one of two tracks—both of which lead to the same place and are shown on the maps. While you're aboard the mine car, stay in a crouched position and blindfire the Lancer at the enemies you encounter. There are no items to pick up, nor is there any steering involved; your job is to make sure Marcus gets to the other end alive.

HANDS AND FEET INSIDE THE VEHICLE!

A brief cutscene plays as Marcus approaches the mine carts. One cart follows the right path, while the other follows the left. These paths intersect twice during the ride, but ending up in the second car puts Marcus further away from the pair of Drones he'll encounter in the main chamber.

CAMPAIGN WALKTHROUGH

The enemies that lurk this section of the mining facility are restricted to one particular place. The mine cars spin and dip at numerous times during the ride, so you might get disoriented. Nevertheless, enemy locations are marked on the accompanying map. So long as Marcus keeps his head down and manages to keep the Dark Wretches from dropping on top of him, he shouldn't have a problem.

LETHIA IMULSION
FACILITY INTERIOR
4 OF 4

START

GET TO THE CORE ROOM

Regardless of which side Marcus and Baird take, the two follow a narrow passage parallel to the one that Dom and Cole follow. Both walkways are the same, each having the same amount of ammunition to pick up and Dark Wretches to kill. The core room is just a short walk away, so get moving.

Grab the Frag Grenades near the entrance to the core room and move into position at the end of the walkway. Anya is in the process of raising the drilling platforms to Delta's position, but that's not all she's raising! Each of the two platforms has a Boomer on it. Ready several Frag Grenades

for the Boomer on the platform near Marcus. Switch to the Lancer to finish it off in case the Frag Grenade merely injures it. Turn to help Dom and Cole deal with their Boomer only after you've killed the one nearest Marcus.

DARKEST BEFORE DAWN

Traverse the caves before the Kryll come home.

START

IMULSION MINES 2

LOCATE THE PUMPING STATION BEFORE DAWN

The drilling platforms don't necessarily let out very close to the pumping station, so Delta Squad has to walk pretty fast to finish the job before the Kryll return. Follow the path leading away from the drilling platforms. Make your way toward the Crimson Omen in the distance. You'll find some Frag Grenades and a COG Tag there.

Return the way you came, and turn right to descend a steep slope toward a collection of steel drums. You can reclaim the Longshot if you swapped it out earlier. The Longshot definitely comes in handy during Marcus' little spelunking episode, so keep it and the Lancer on hand until we advise otherwise.

Return up the slope with the Lancer in hand and flatten the approaching Dark Wretches. There are only eight of them, but it's enough to make Marcus instruct Baird and Cole to stay behind and guard the resonator—it's just Marcus and Dom from here on out.

CAMPAIGN
WALKTHROUGH

COG TAG #22

This COG Tag is on the ground in front of the Crimson Omen, not far from the drilling platforms you ride down into the mine.

Keep moving, and fight through the second wave of Dark Wretches en route to the ledge overlooking the water fall. It's time to take another ride! Marcus and Dom slide down an impossibly slippery slope to a lower level of the mine.

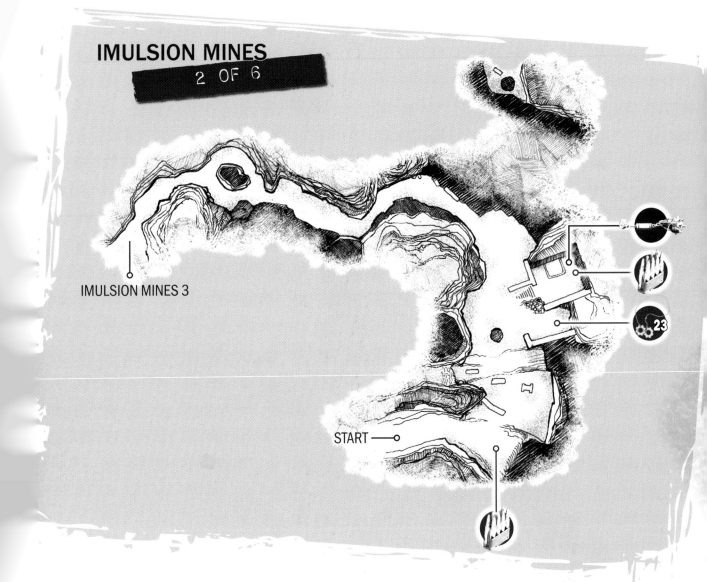

IMULSION MINES 3

START

REGROUP WITH BAIRD AND GUS

Cross the bloody river and take cover behind the rocks ahead. A small squad of Grenadiers and Drones rapidly approach from a position near the structure on the right. Focus on the Grenadier on the right first, as he tries to rush Marcus and Dom's position. Once he's out of commission, use the Longshot to pick off the Drones one by one.

Proceed past the structure and note the weakened column across the chasm to the right. A Sniper has moved into position on that ledge under the column. Marcus can either use the Longshot to snipe the Sniper or use the Lancer to shoot the column, depositing several tons of rock on him. Proceed deeper into the mines.

COG TAG #23

Approach the area to the right of the stairs that lead up to the small structure. The COG Tag is on the ground near the wall.

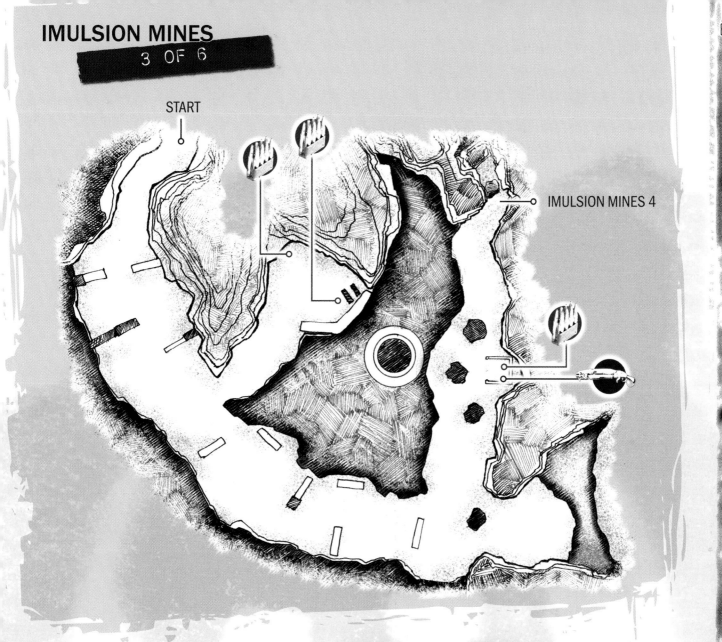

START

IMULSION MINES 4

Fight past the smattering of Dark Wretches ahead, and move into position behind the cover on the left. A Boomer fires his massive Boomshot from across a small canyon in the distance. Shoulder the Longshot and hit him with two or three bullets to the head. Manage this, and the next "boom" you'll hear will be his massive derriere slamming to the ground.

Gather the ammo from this cave section's side areas and continue to the left. Marcus and Dom soon take another nasty spill, this time down the chute of a grub hole. A call into Baird reveals Marcus isn't the only one lost.

CAMPAIGN
WALKTHROUGH

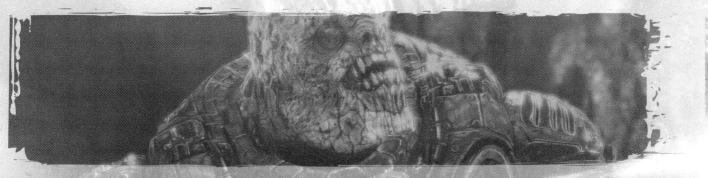

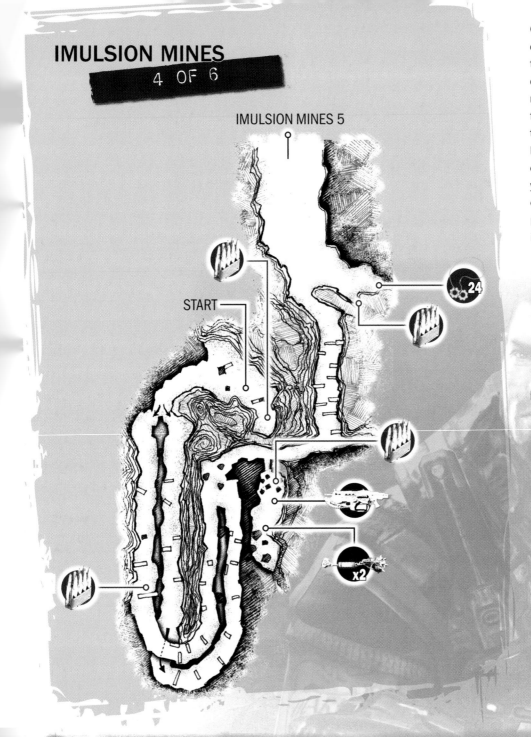

IMULSION MINES 5

START

x2

24

Give Dom the "Attack" command and work together to slaughter the fifteen or so Dark Wretches that rush forward. There's a fork in the road just beyond the fracas with the mine's lambent critters. Regardless of the path you choose, you have the good fortune of always being in close proximity to Dom, as he isn't far away.

RIGHT PATH: HIGH ROUTE

Marcus and Dom may be on separate paths, but they're within eyesight of one another the entire time they're apart. It's not long before the first wave of Dark Wretches rushes forward. Backpedal as you use the Lancer or Gnasher to spray them with lead. Whenever Marcus' immediate area is clear of enemies, take a quick look to the left to give Dom a hand. There are a couple of Drones mixed in with the Dark Wretches, so expect some gunfire. The last of the enemies is likely to be the Drone on the distant left side. If you're still carrying the Longshot, use it to snipe him so that Dom can push on.

The two rocky paths crisscross up ahead. Keep moving, making a mental note that Dom is now on the right. Cut a path through the Dark Wretches, Drones, and Grenadiers up ahead. The Grenadiers try to utilize the available cover, sometimes even moving into position opposite Marcus against the same object. When this happens, utilize blindfire or even the Lancer's chainsaw bayonet to slay them. Regroup with Dom up ahead.

LEFT PATH: LOW ROUTE

Allow Dom to get ahead of Marcus, and listen closely for the sound of the Locust battlecry. Quickly draw the Longshot and snipe the Drone rushing toward Dom on the right path. Switch back to the Lancer and mow down the Dark Wretches closing in around Marcus. Keep tabs on Dom's position, and use the Lancer to give him a hand whenever you can, as the Dark Wretches may overwhelm him.

The two paths crisscross ahead, and the trail Marcus is on dips under a stone archway. Use the Longshot to put down the Drone beneath this arch and keep moving.

There are several more Drones and another dozen or so Dark Wretches split between the two paths up ahead. Move to the first piece of cover when you hear the Locust bellow, and employ the Longshot against them. Clear out the nearby Dark Wretches before you suppress the Drones near Dom's position. This gives him time to rush in with the chainsaw bayonet. Regroup with Dom up ahead.

Approach the edge of the walkway. Land a Frag Grenade on the nearby rock ledge. The resulting blast causes the nearby rock ledge to crumble, thereby giving Marcus a way down to the platform. Gather the ammo and Frag Grenades amongst the chunks of Wretch flesh, and continue your journey.

The pathway ahead has many pieces of cover for Marcus and Dom to use as they fight through a throng of Drones and Dark Wretches. The battle kicks off with a Grenadier rushing forward. Stay behind cover until he's in view, and then cut him open with the chainsaw bayonet. Next up is the Dark Wretches. Ignore the distant Drones for the time being. Instead, lure the Dark Wretches back around the corner so you're out of view from the Drones. Once you eliminate the Dark Wretches, move back into cover and advance slowly alongside Dom, allowing him to suppress the enemies while you ready the Longshot.

COG TAG #24

Follow the cave's right edge to the narrow ledge over the massive Imulsion pool. The COG Tag is off the main path, and you must turn around to find it.

ANGRY TITAN

David versus Goliath.

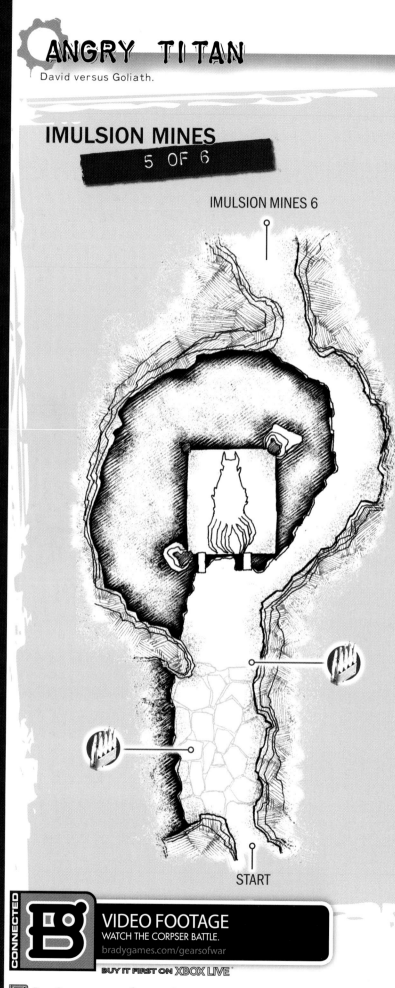

IMULSION MINES 6

START

ACT

3

BELLY OF THE BEAST

KILL THE CORPSER

The Corpser has lurked in the distance everywhere Marcus and the others have gone, but it has always fled without confrontation...until now. Delta Squad has entered the Imulsion mines, the home of the Corpser, and there is no going back. It's either kill or be killed.

Marcus and Dom battle the Corpser atop a series of floating rock slabs in an otherwise deadly pool of Imulsion. Although these rock chunks can support the Corpser's weight, they crumble and sink with a particularly powerful jab from its mighty claws. As these blocks sink, Marcus and Dom lose the ability to keep a safe distance from the Corpser.

Fortunately for Marcus, the gigantic Corpser is not without weakness; it's possible to kill it somewhat quickly. Equip the Lancer and stand in the middle of the floating battleground. Wait for the Corpser to lift several of its claws. The Corpser raises its claws into the air before striking down at Marcus or Dom. The key is to get close enough to the Corpser so that the claws come down behind them.

While the claws are raised, use the Lancer to target the Corpser's soft belly. Aim for the area just above what appears to be a metallic belt. Hit it in the stomach with half a clip of ammo to inflict enough pain that it rears up and begins to scream. Now it's time to strike! Quickly raise the Lancer's barrel and shoot the Corpser in its open mouth. Aim for the lower jaw to avoid its protective outer layer. When you successfully hit the Corpser in the mouth, it retreats a few steps.

DARK WRETCHES ARE COMING!

Once you hit the Corpser in the mouth and it backs up a few steps, several Dark Wretches enter the fray. Although they pose an additional threat, the following tips help you kill the Corpser so fast that the Dark Wretches don't get a chance to join the fun.

The Corpser strikes with its claws in several ways. When it raises three claws, it attacks at a distance with each one individually. This attack is easy to avoid, as the attack's focus is to destroy the floating rock slabs behind Marcus and Dom. When it spreads its claws really wide, Marcus should expect it to strike hard with its middle claws at close range—this attack will likely kill Marcus if it hits him. The third attack is less predictable. The Corpser spreads its claws out in a sudden jabbing motion as it lets loose a powerful scream. This attack simply knocks Marcus backward and stuns him, but it's not fatal.

The best way to kill the Corpser is to move to the area's far left side and get within a couple steps of the Corpser's claws. To make the Corpser rear up, use the Lancer to shoot between its side claws. Then quickly shoot it in the mouth. Run after the Corpser, keeping to the left, and repeat this process a second and a third time. Once the Corpser retreats to the wooden platform in the Imulsion pool's center, use the Lancer to shoot off the two clamps holding the platform to solid ground (use the Y Button to pinpoint their location when the prompt appears). If you follow these tactics, you can kill the Corpser and be on your way in well under a minute.

IMULSION MINES
6 OF 6

START

SECURE THE PUMPING STATION

Baird and Cole made their way to the rear of the Corpser's location and have the resonator intact. Proceed onto the narrow path across the Imulsion, and locate the **Torquebow** at the base of the cliff to the right.

TORQUEBOW USAGE

The Torquebow is an especially powerful weapon in that it allows its user to fire an explosive charge a great distance with pinpoint accuracy. Not only that, but unlike the Frag Grenade, the Torquebow's arrows stick into whatever they hit—even members of the Locust Horde! Although the arrows explode roughly two seconds after they're fired, it's possible for a struck enemy to inadvertently deliver the explosive charge within range of his teammates. However, you must hold back the bowstring long enough to get sufficient tension for the arrow to penetrate its target. The longer you hold the R Trigger, the straighter and farther the arrow flies upon release. Speaking of which, you can't hold the R Trigger indefinitely, as the Torquebow self-fires after eight seconds of aiming.

Within sight of the pumping station, Marcus instructs Baird and Cole to flank to the right while he and Dom storm the front. Move from cover to cover along the pumping station's left side.

As the duo gets closer, they realize that Theron Guards defend the pumping station. Unlike standard Drones, Theron Guards are faster, stronger, and much, much smarter. They're also equipped with Torquebows and Gnasher shotguns (they sometimes even have Lancers). Theron Guards are very good at using cover and, overall, they're simply harder to kill.

Duck for cover behind the short wall that parallels the pump station. Use a Frag Grenade to flush out the first wave of Theron Guards. Now switch to the Torquebow and hit the Theron Guards with the explosive arrows. Marcus and Dom can take out over a half-dozen Theron Guards from this vantage point. Once the Locust stop coming, go around to the front of the pumping station to regroup with Baird and Cole. It's time to put the Lancer to use!

Make your way to the near-side ramp that leads up to the pumping station walkway. More than likely, a couple of Theron Guards and a Grenadier will be there to greet you. Use the chainsaw bayonet or a Frag Grenade to slice through them, and pick up any extra Torquebow ammunition from the corpses. Take cover on the right and peer around the corner to spot the Theron Guards in the distance. There may be as few as one or two or as many as three or four. Either way, use the Torquebow to thin the herd, and gradually advance toward the far side of the platform. Issue the "Attack" command to get the others to join in your counter-clockwise sweep of the pumping station.

DON'T DUEL WITH EXPLOSIVES!

Theron Guards are not stupid. If you see one off in the distance seemingly standing still and staring at you, don't stare back. You may think you have time to raise the Torquebow and shoot him, but what you don't realize is that he's already in the process of doing the same to you! By the time you release a shot, you'll have an explosive arrow stuck in your armor and you'll be dead before you know it.

RESTORE POWER TO THE ELEVATOR

Once you've won the battle and secured the pumping station, cross the bridge toward the power column near the path that Baird and Cole took. Press the green button to start the elevator. Baird and Cole deploy the resonator. Good job, men!

ACT 4: THE LONG ROAD HOME

THE LONG ROAD HOME

ACT

4

SITUATION REPORT

He had him sent to prison. He left him for dead when the Locust Horde invaded. Hoffman did all these things and more to Marcus, yet never had Marcus hated the sound of Hoffman's voice more than when he radioed to say the resonator didn't work. The blast wasn't powerful enough to map even a fraction of the Locust tunnel network—the crew would need to find another way, and Baird thinks he has the solution. He hacked into a geobot and found an immense amount of data concerning the Locust tunnels. Anya has traced the data back to the residence of Adam Fenix, Marcus' deceased father. The irony in Hoffman sending Marcus there to look for additional data isn't lost on the members of Delta Squad.

COG TAGS

25
Beside the stairs going up to the building on the right near the starting point.

26
Behind the burned-out car across from the conservatory's pillars.

27
The COG Tag is under the desk in the library on the mansion's first floor.

CAMPUS GRINDER

Bullies on the playground.

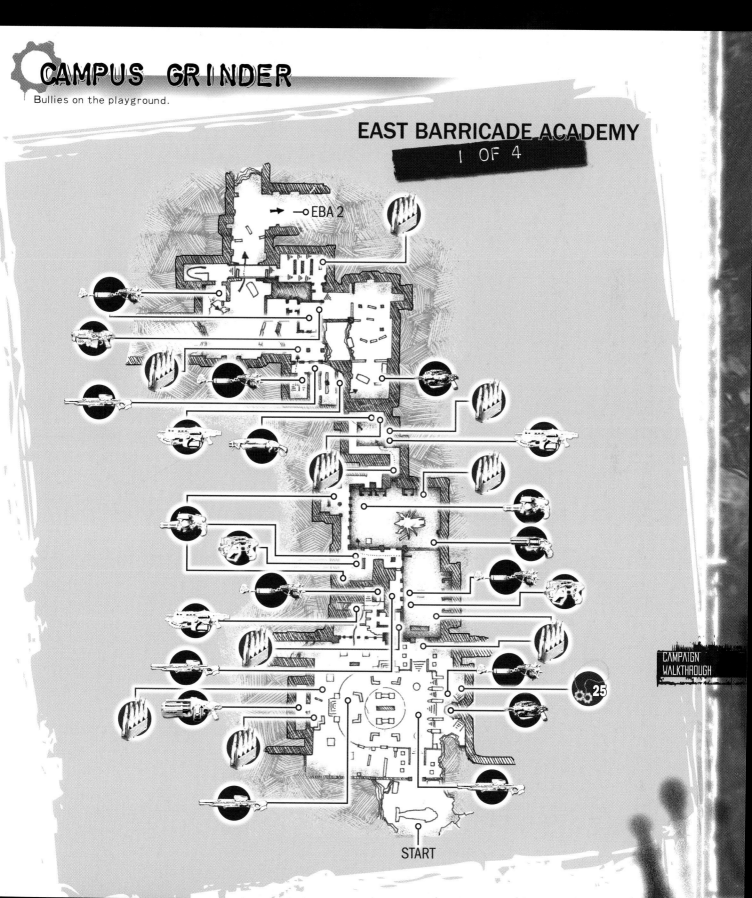

EAST BARRICADE ACADEMY
1 OF 4

→─○ EBA 2

25

CAMPAIGN WALKTHROUGH

START

SECURE THE CONTEMPORARY COMBAT CENTER

The large campus courtyard just beyond the landing zone is overrun with Locust—they knew Marcus was coming and amassed an impressive counteroffensive. The first wave of Grenadiers and Drones emerges from the building to the far left. This is where Dom, Baird, and Cole go, but this is not where Marcus should go. Instead, flank to the right and take cover near the stairs to the building on the right. From there, use the Torquebow and/or Longshot to assist the other Delta Squad members from long range.

The second Locust wave emerges from the building near Marcus' position. Have Frag Grenades and the Lancer ready to deal with the Grenadiers and Theron Guard as they emerge from the closed doors near the stairs. Circle around the walls near the steps to maintain adequate cover. Most of all, don't be afraid to use the chainsaw bayonet against a Theron Guard.

COG TAG #25

From the starting point, go to the right and look on the ground near the short staircases that lead to the dormitory on that side of the campus quad.

Once you eliminate the enemies emerging from the building near Marcus, a third wave attacks. This wave contains several Grenadiers and a pair of Boomers. Use the Torquebow and Lancer to cut down the Boomers; stay near that same location to the right. Use the cover to stay alive, and continue using long-range weapons against the Boomers.

Once you've defeated the final Locust, take a moment to collect ammo and weaponry from the battlefield. Anya lets the squad know that there are survivors from the chopper that crashed, and, like any good soldier, Marcus decides at once to help them. This means the crew has to split up.

RIGHT PATH: STREET LEVEL

INVESTIGATE THE DOWNED CHOPPER

Taking the right path is not an easy option, as it puts Marcus and Baird in direct contact with a sizable portion of the Locust Horde. Fortunately, Cole and Dom have the drop on many of the enemies and provide cover from the second floor of the building interior.

Enter the courtyard near the statue and immediately take cover behind the large pillar. Several Grenadiers emerge from cover to the right. With Dom's elevated support, use the Torquebow or a Frag Grenade to take them out, and then move to the left. Several Theron Guards move in from that side of the courtyard, so be prepared. Have the Torquebow ready to fire into the area's left-rear corner. During this battle, the Theron Guards and Grenadiers try to rush Marcus and Baird's position, so don't advance. Use the Torquebow to keep them at bay, and switch to the Lancer if they get close. The chainsaw bayonet beats them back quickly.

ARROWS OVER HAMMER

Be sure to swap out the Hammer of Dawn in favor of the Torquebow once you've neutralized the threat in this area. There aren't any Seeders or Berserkers for quite a while, and the Torquebow is just too good to leave lying on the sidewalk. Besides, the Theron Guard corpses in this area offer a steady supply of ammo for the Torquebow.

Move through the hallway to the left to enter the next courtyard. There, Marcus and Baird come face-to-face with a Seeder. Anya points out the Hammer of Dawn on the sidewalk to the left, but several Locust guard it. Use the Torquebow to eliminate the Grenadier behind the statue in the back-left corner, and dodge the Nemacysts on the way to gather the Hammer of Dawn. Baird and the others help keep the Nemacysts off Marcus long enough to kill the Seeder.

The moment the Seeder is killed, ready a Frag Grenade to throw into the ankh-shaped statue between the park benches, as an Emergence Hole is set to open. Close the hole, then get into the alcove in the left corner (near the Hammer of Dawn's original location). Issue the "Attack" command so that Baird, Dom, and Cole help eliminate the Locust that succeed in emerging from the hole.

Proceed through the building to the left's empty hallways and out into the street in the distance. Kill the Wretches that come hopping toward Marcus, and move into cover near the two small barricades. Use the Torquebow to kill the Drones in the street beyond the wall. Many more Wretches attack, but Marcus can put them down using the Torquebow as a melee weapon—after all, there's a reason that the bow's limbs are bladed!

CAMPAIGN WALKTHROUGH

Marcus and Baird may be in the clear for the time being, but it's time for them to repay the favor to Dom and Cole. There are several Locust across the chasm in the street to the left. They have Cole pinned down pretty good. Take cover behind the bombed-out car and use Frag Grenades and the Torquebow to eliminate them. Additional reinforcements arrive from the building across from Cole and Dom. Move into the small yard up ahead to the left, and throw some Frag Grenades through the windows to further reduce their numbers. Once Marcus and Baird have done all they can, lead them inside the lecture hall and load up on the ammunition near the podium.

Fight your way outside the top of the lecture hall and across the walkway to the other building. Dom requests assistance with the Gunner who has them pinned down with the Troika on the lower level. Don't try to take out

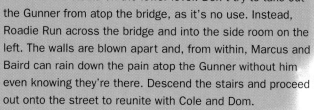

the Gunner from atop the bridge, as it's no use. Instead, Roadie Run across the bridge and into the side room on the left. The walls are blown apart and, from within, Marcus and Baird can rain down the pain atop the Gunner without him even knowing they're there. Descend the stairs and proceed out onto the street to reunite with Cole and Dom.

LEFT PATH: THROUGH THE BUILDINGS

The route through the buildings places Marcus and Baird in perfect position to provide sniper support from an elevated perch.

Make your way into the building and take cover near the lockers. A Theron Guard is around the corner up ahead. Theron Guards use their Torquebows in nearly every situation, so rush this one's position between shots and chainsaw it to death.

The wall ahead is blown out, providing a perfect view of the small courtyard to the right. This is rather fortunate, as Dom and Cole are under heavy fire. Assist Delta Two by using the Longshot to snipe the Theron Guards and Grenadiers down below.

Continue down the hall to the next room. Use the Lancer to cut down the initial wave of Wretches and the Grenadier that appears near the lockers. Then turn your attention to the Seeder down below. Snipe any Grenadiers and Theron Guards you see, then swap out the Longshot for any of the three Hammers of Dawn scattered around the upstairs area. Use the walls and debris for cover from the Nemacysts while you work to kill the Seeder.

Switch to the Frag Grenades the second the Seeder is destroyed. Look toward the obelisk-like statue in the center of the yard. Toss the Frag Grenade the second the Emergence Hole opens under the statue, then grab the Lancer and beat back the next batch of Wretches that appear near the lockers. Help Baird finish off any Theron Guards lurking in the courtyard below, and then move on.

Use the wheel up ahead to raise the gates. This allows Marcus and Baird to continue through the building. Plus, Cole and Dom won't be locked in the courtyard anymore. Head through the balcony overlooking the small classroom, and proceed onto the ruined second floor near the broken toilet ahead.

Use the Longshot to take out the Sniper in the building cattycorner from the toilet. Then lend your marksman skills to Dom and Cole by shooting the Locust in the street below and to the right.

Descend the stairs to street level and snipe the Locust in the building across the street—look for one near the wall to the right and the other in the doorway straight ahead. Cut through the building across the street to reach the cordoned-off area to the left. Take cover from the Troika near the barricade, and use a Frag Grenade to kill the Gunner if Dom and Cole don't get to him fast enough. Hurdle the barricade and check the stairwell beyond the Troika for any surviving Locust. When the last of them are defeated, Dom and Cole rejoin the team in the street below.

The downed chopper is straight ahead. Shoot the propane tanks near the gate to blow it open. Hurry over to the survivors before the Stranded pick the bodies clean of weaponry.

BAD TO WORSE

Enjoy the local flora and fauna.

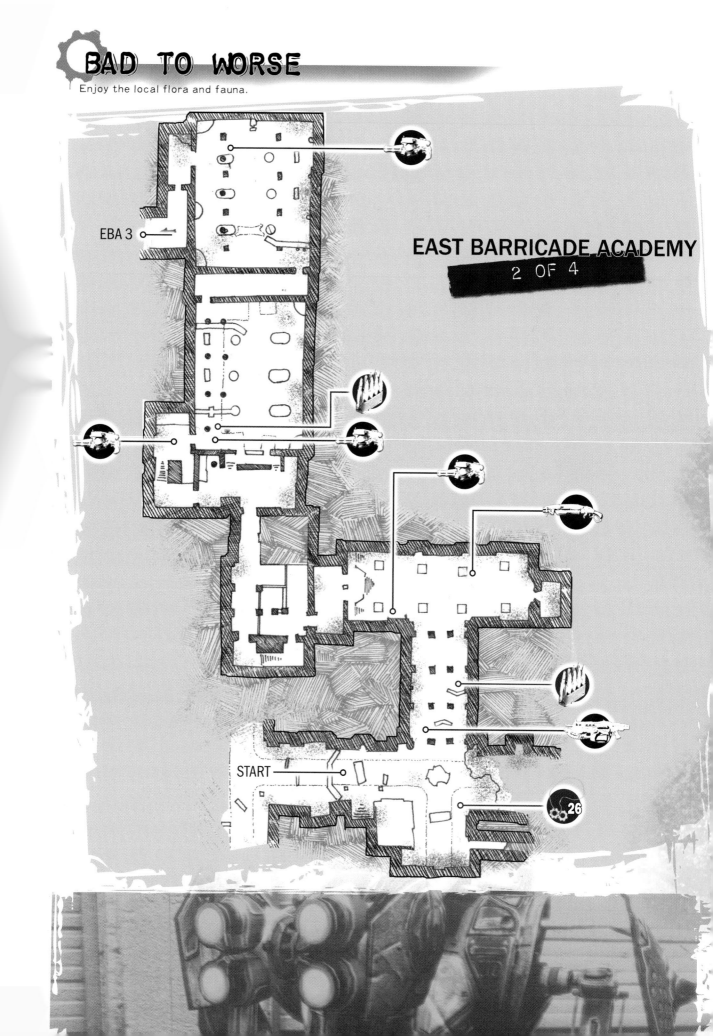

EBA 3

START

26

TRAVEL TO THE CONSERVATORY

COG TAG #26

This COG Tag is on the sidewalk, behind the rusted car that's across from the columned walkway that leads to the conservatory entrance.

The conservatory entrance is ahead to the left. Proceed to the yard ahead along the pathway with the pillars, and grab the Hammer of Dawn lying on the ground to the left. The metal door leading into the conservatory requires Jack's handiwork to open, and that means only one thing! It's time to kill some Locust!

DEFEND JACK UNTIL THE DOORS OPEN

Equip the Frag Grenades and hurry back the way you came to the street outside. If you Roadie Run fast enough, you just might get there before the Emergence Hole opens! Use the Frag Grenade to shut the hole. Then lob another one to reduce the number of enemies that escaped before it closed. A pair of Boomers blows a hole through the brick wall at the end of the yard opposite Jack!

Rush back to Jack's defense and equip the Hammer of Dawn you picked up moments ago. Use the Hammer of Dawn against the Boomers, making sure to keep track of both Boomers' positions. The quicker you make it back to them after sealing off the Emergence Hole, the better chance you have of keeping them grouped together. Whatever you do, don't poke your head out from behind cover when you hear one of them yell, "Boom!"

PROCEED THROUGH THE CONSERVATORY

Hold onto the Hammer of Dawn and enter the conservatory. The heavy steel doors on the outside did a good job keeping the Locust from entering, so Marcus can enjoy the serenity of the area and take a relaxed look around.

Climb the stairs to the left, and then step out onto the balconies overlooking the arboretum ahead. Descend the stairs to the left and continue out into the first of the two arboretums.

As Marcus and Dom reach the door at the end of this first arboretum, they come face-to-face with another Berserker! Lure the Berserker away from the door and then rush through it. She crashes through the wall into the hallway connecting the two arboretums, but she's easy to slip past. Continue to the room ahead, where the Berserker again crashes through the wall. The only difference is that there's no way out of this room just yet! Not only does Marcus have to kill the Berserker, but he also has to use her to bash a way out.

5 MINUTES OF SATELLITE COVERAGE

The timer on the screen indicates how much time Marcus has to use the Hammer of Dawn. Note that the Hammer of Dawn can be used even after the Berserker is destroyed. It's a good thing too, as there are some pretty hard-to-kill Locust outside the arboretum. Kill the Berserker as fast as you can, then rush outside without delay.

The problem with using the Hammer of Dawn on the Berserker is that you need an open view of the sky to do it. Fortunately, the seven stone pillars located between each of the planters are connected to the glass roof above. By luring the Berserker toward these pillars, Marcus can use the Berserker to destroy the roof, thereby allowing the satellites to get a fix on the Hammer of Dawn's targeting reticule.

Rev the Lancer's chainsaw bayonet to attract the Berserker toward each of the stone pillars. Stand on the side of the pillar opposite the Berserker, rev the chainsaw to get her attention, then dive out of the way as she comes crashing through the stone. This destroys the roof's supports, allowing Marcus to use the Hammer of Dawn. The third pillar on the left (as viewed from entering the room) actually topples over instead of breaking apart—in doing so, it crashes through a wall and starts a small fire.

Ignore the fire for now. Continue coaxing the Berserker into breaking the pillars, and then kill her with three lengthy Hammer of Dawn blasts. Once she's dead, rush to the rear wall and turn the large valve to extinguish the fire. With the fire out, climb through the rubble and kick open the door to exit the conservatory.

HAZING

Surprise encore.

EAST BARRICADE ACADEMY
3 OF 4

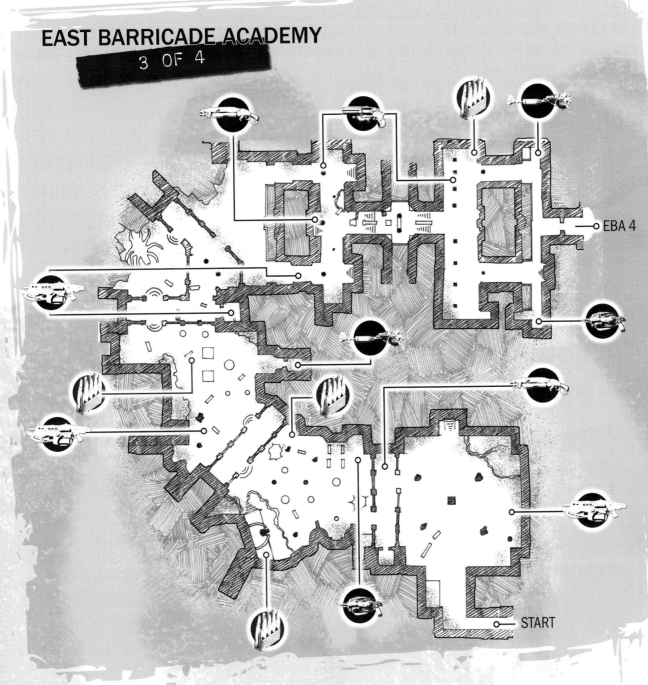

EBA 4

START

PROCEED TOWARD THE FENIX ESTATE

There will be plenty of time to search the courtyard and hallway ahead for weapons and ammo in a minute. But first, take advantage of the satellite coverage and put the Hammer of Dawn to use! Rush through the short hallway to the second courtyard and take cover on the left.

Use the Hammer of Dawn to eliminate the Troika Gunner and Spotter behind the sandbags in the distance. Take out any other Locust in the vicinity, then move to the yard's center and turn back toward the direction from which you came—an Emergence Hole soon opens. Use the Hammer of Dawn to eviscerate the Locust as they reach the surface. This will likely close the hole as well. A second Emergence Hole opens to the right of the Troika, so be ready. If you managed to defeat the Berserker quickly enough, there should be plenty of time to secure this courtyard with the Hammer of Dawn.

Grab the Torquebow from the courtyard and move through the next hallway to the third yard. There, a Theron Guard appears on the roof amongst several Nemacysts. Don't worry about trying to kill the Theron, as it can't be killed. Instead, focus on eliminating the three Nemacysts before they dive-bomb Marcus and Dom.

Once you eliminate the Nemacysts, take cover near the planters in the center of the yard. The first wave of Drones attacks from the left. The second wave drops from the windows above the area to the right. Utilize cover and look for opportunities to score multiple kills with a single Torquebow arrow. Lastly, a Boomer marches its way out of the next corridor. Use the Torquebow and Lancer to cut it down.

METAL VERSUS WOOD

Notice something different about the boarded-up doors? Some are covered with unbreakable metal, but others are covered with wood, which is not nearly as impenetrable. For example, inspect the door atop the stairs in the third courtyard (after you kill the Boomer). Notice the wooden boards. Shoot these boards with the Lancer to knock them off. Marcus can then kick open the door to find some extra Frag Grenades. Remember that not all barriers are solid.

Bypass the corpse of the Seeder and continue through the corridor to the building's exterior. From here, the path forks to go around the building and rejoins on the other side. Regardless which way Marcus loops around the building, he ends up at the entrance to a narrow alley guarded by Locust.

Take cover near the large, stone blocks and use Frag Grenades to reduce the initial enemy numbers. Several Grenadiers try to rush Marcus and Dom's position, so keep a watchful eye for signs of movement. Use the Lancer to cut down the Grenadiers before they get close enough to strike with their potent Gnashers. Finally, a Booomer descends the alley steps and attacks at close range. Use the Lancer to weaken him as he approaches, then retreat to the top of the stairs opposite the alley. Grab the Gnasher located there. Move back into position behind the blocks below. Blow a hole in the Boomer's face with a steady barrage of blindfire. If you don't want to use the Gnasher, the Boltok Pistol makes a good alternative.

ACTIVE RELOAD OFTEN

The battles are really starting to increase in intensity and, as you may have guessed, the ability to reload quickly and often is a valuable habit. While making sure your weapon is always fully loaded is a good idea, it's even more beneficial to achieve perfect Active Reloads, as the blinking bullets in the magazine dish out increased damage. This is a great way to enhance less powerful weapons when you're dealing with Boomers.

Continue around the next campus building to the sidewalk on the other side, which leads toward the campus' waterfront section. Grab the Torquebow behind the wooden dresser in the alley before you leave the primary campus area.

CLOSE TO HOME
Academy campus uprising.

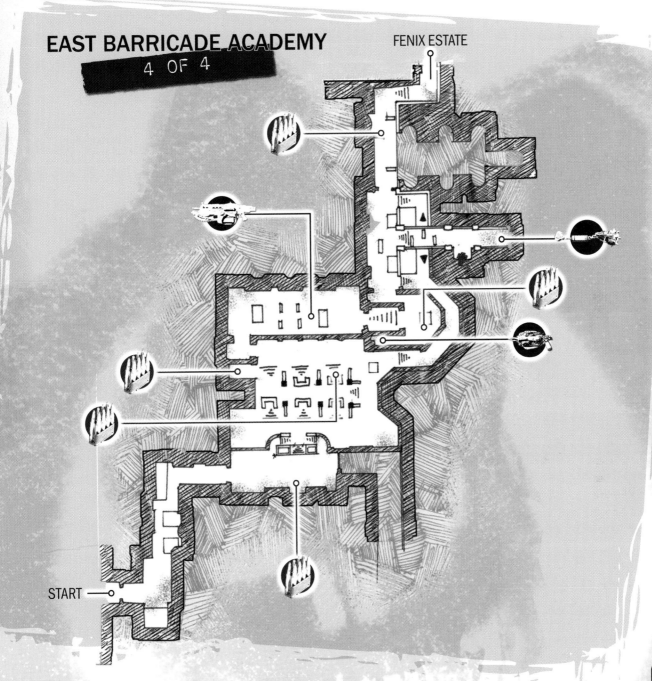

EAST BARRICADE ACADEMY
4 OF 4

FENIX ESTATE

START

PROCEED TOWARD THE FENIX ESTATE

Equip the Torquebow and slide into cover alongside the wall overlooking the garden. There are roughly eight Drones, Grenadiers, and Theron Guards in this area. Use the Torquebow to kill as many as you can spot from behind the wall above the garden. Then, with support from Dom and his Lancer, descend the steps and finish off the rest at close range. Dom does a good job pinning down the final one or two enemies, thereby giving Marcus an opportunity to sneak up behind them and put the chainsaw bayonet to use.

Cross the covered garden area and follow the right path out onto the stone walkway near the water. Stay close to the left wall and ready the Torquebow. Quickly sidestep out into enemy fire and loose a Torquebow arrow at the Troika on the bridge—ignore the Drones behind the sandbags for now. Duck back into cover and ready a second arrow. Use this one to destroy the Gunner manning the Troika located under the bridge. The walkway crumbles if Marcus tries to advance along this route, so double back through the garden and follow the path toward the cemetery to the left.

WHERE'S DOM?

Dom automatically follows the route Marcus doesn't choose. This is another reason why it's good for Marcus to move along the waterfront first, as that area provides little cover and Dom may well get shot up. Should Dom be downed, hurry to revive him.

Fight through the gang of Grenadiers and Drones near the headstones, and continue to the walkway ahead. Loop around to the right to take the Torquebow from the COG corpse. Move into position closer to the

bridge, where you can use it to eliminate the remaining Locust. Use Frag Grenades to flush out the Grenadiers from behind the sandbag barricades on the walkway near the bridge. Finish them off with the Gnasher. Collect the dropped weapons and Frag Grenades from the bridge, and continue toward the Fenix Estate, which is just ahead.

IMAGINARY PLACE
Storm the House!

FENIX ESTATE 2

ADAM FENIX'S ESTATE
1 OF 4

START

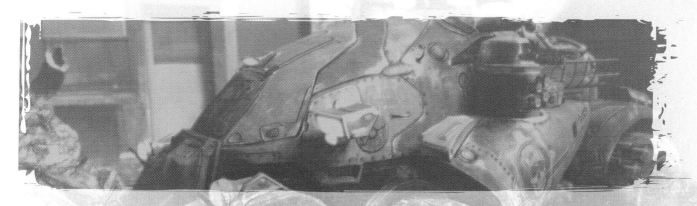

GAIN ENTRANCE TO THE FENIX ESTATE

The entrance to the Fenix Estate via the East Barricade Academy leads through a sculpture garden and up numerous flights of stairs to a manicured courtyard. As Marcus undoubtedly expected, there are Theron Guards and a Grenadier positioned on the stairs—they have superior numbers and an elevated position.

Rush up the left-side stairs to the first landing. Dom follows Marcus' lead, moving up the right-side stairs to lend fire support. Use the Lancer and Torquebow to finish off the Grenadier on the upper landing, as well as the Theron Guard near the statue above. but listen closely for the throaty bellows of an approaching Boomer. Stay in cover as you ready the Torquebow. Briefly lean out and let the arrow fly. With Dom's assistance and an accurate shot, it shouldn't take much to finish off the Boomer.

Gather the ammo and weapons and climb the stairs to the courtyard doors. Baird and Cole meet Marcus inside the left door. Although the foursome is currently pinned down by Drones in the house's upper floor, Baird has some good news. There's an APC out back, and he thinks he knows how to fix it. Baird and Cole lure the Drones away when they make a dash for the back of the house. Now it's time for Marcus and Dom to head inside.

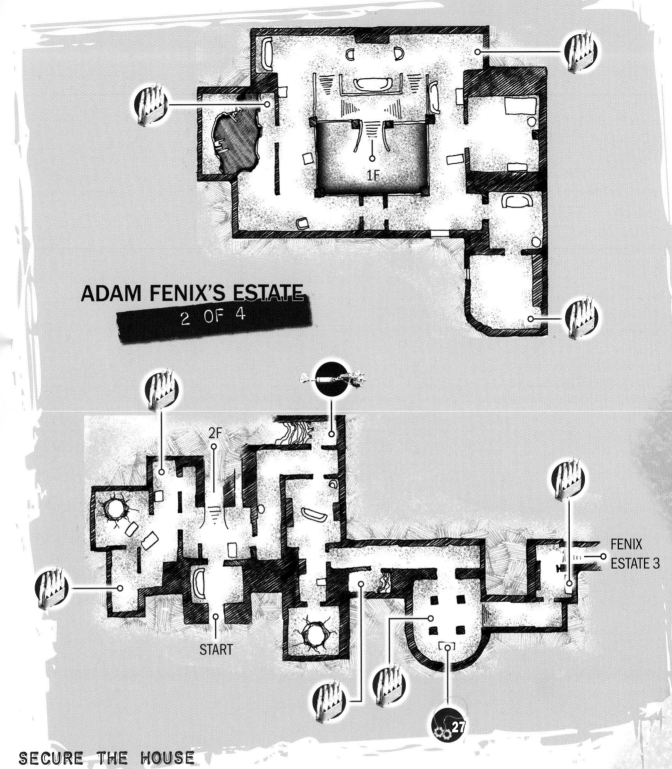

ADAM FENIX'S ESTATE

1F

2F

FENIX
ESTATE 3

START

27

SECURE THE HOUSE

Ready a Frag Grenade and cross the entrance room at an angle to the left. As soon as Marcus passes the stairway, an Emergence Hole opens in the room's back-left corner, so get ready to close it.

LOCKED DOORS

The two doors on the foyer's right side are currently sealed with unbreakable metal sheeting. The Locust open these doors soon enough, so note their position and search the rest of the house.

With the Emergence Hole sealed off, ascend the right set of stairs and approach the fireplace in the center with another Frag Grenade in hand. Several Grenadiers emerge from the room to the left (the one above the Emergence Hole's location). A good Frag Grenade toss should eliminate at least half of the Grenadiers. Use the Lancer to finish off the rest from across the room. But remember that the couches and chairs offer only temporary cover—they are highly destructible!

Dom announces when the upstairs is clear of Locust. Take a minute to get the lay of the floor and gather the Frag Grenades that the Grenadiers dropped. It's time to return downstairs.

Watch for the solitary Grenadier to burst through the door near the entrance. Gun him down and then proceed through the hall beyond that doorway with a Frag Grenade in hand. A rather large Emergence Hole is about to open in the room at the end of the corridor around the corner. Rush forward and take cover near the room's entrance, and close the hole with a Frag Grenade. Quickly switch to the Torquebow to eliminate any surviving Locust in there. Continue across this level of the house to reach the wine cellar's entrance. Marcus must crank open the gate via the wheel on the wall to proceed.

COG TAG #27

Enter the oval-shaped library on the first floor and use the chainsaw bayonet to destroy the desk. The COG Tag is on the floor under the desk.

ADAM FENIX'S ESTATE
3 OF 4

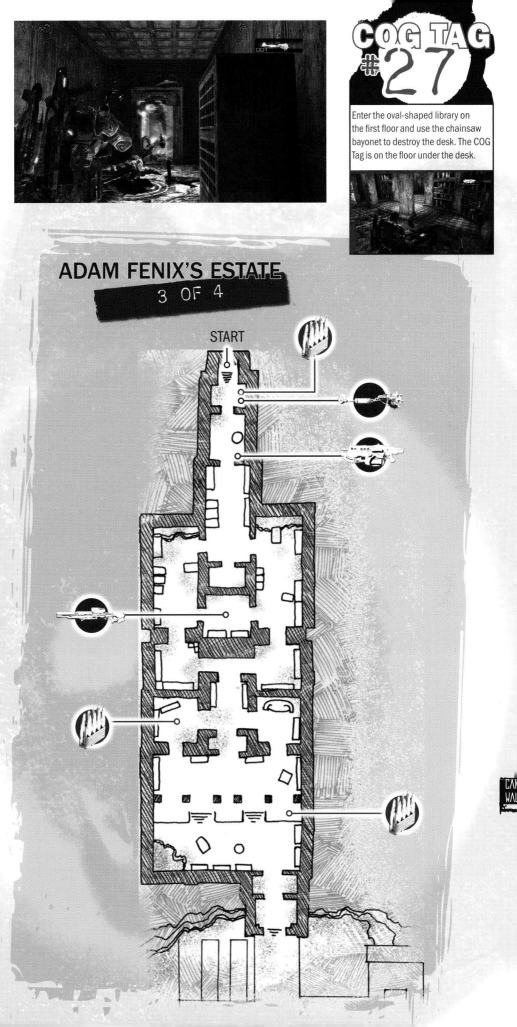

START

CAMPAIGN WALKTHROUGH

SEARCH THE BASEMENT FOR THE HIDDEN LAB

If the data found in the geobot truly originated from this location, then Marcus' father must have had a secret laboratory somewhere in the basement. Saw through the wooden boards on the first landing to get the Frag Grenades, and continue down the stairs to the basement.

Stop on the last landing before you reach the basement. Lob a Frag Grenade into the room beyond the stairs to eliminate the two Drones located there. Kick open the door to the wine cellar and proceed toward the rear of the area. Refrain from picking up the Longshot in the center area for now, unless Marcus is low on Torquebow arrows. By the time Marcus reaches the rear area, Baird radios to let him know the APC is up and running.

There are numerous wine racks, but the one all the way to the left along the back wall is the only one with a wooden doorframe around it. Approach this wine rack and press the X Button to kick it open. Unfortunately, there is a locked metal door directly behind it that requires Jack's assistance. That could mean only one thing...

ENTRENCHED
Evict the Locust from Adam's house.

PROTECT JACK WHILE HE OPENS THE LAB DOOR

Take cover behind the nearby wall, facing the gate in the center of the cellar. Ready a Frag Grenade and/or the Torquebow and let the explosives fly as soon as the Drones and Grenadiers appear. There are six of them, and the explosives should wipe out the first three or four. Watch for a Grenadier that tries to flank Marcus from the left. Others try to move in for cover behind the nearby pillars. This is close enough to Marcus' position that he can cut them down with some well-placed blindfire.

SEARCH THE LAB

Return to Jack's location and enter the lab. Inside, Marcus locates the data that Anya was hoping—and fearing—to get. Turns out that the resonator's data *did* reveal only a minute fraction of the Locust tunnel network. Unfortunately, the data files are simply too big for Anya to transfer over the network; Jack has to download them. But it's going to take time, and time is one thing that Delta Squad doesn't have to waste.

REGROUP AT THE FRONT OF THE HOUSE

Baird and Cole are in dire need of assistance, as a platoon of Locust advances toward the mansion's front door. They can't hold them off much longer without some help. Use the Lancer to cut a path through the Wretches and Grenadier that make their way into the cellar, and return to the house's main floor. Collect any ammo you see along the way, but don't waste time.

A Drone locks the double doors leading out of the library, thus trapping Dom and Marcus inside with a dozen hungry Wretches. Circle-strafe around the room's perimeter and use the Lancer to put them away. Once you defeat the last Wretch, the Drone kicks open the door and starts firing. Be there to let loose the chainsaw bayonet when he does.

Rush back through the house to the main entryway, and climb the stairs to the second floor where Baird and Cole are waiting. There are a number of Theron Guards, Drones, and Grenadiers in the courtyard outside—Baird and Cole leave them for Dom and Marcus while they go around back to protect the APC.

DEFEND THE FRONT OF THE HOUSE

Head toward the room that's to the left of where Baird was hunkered down. Use the blown-out wall to get the drop on a group of enemies. From this vantage point, a well-aimed Torquebow arrow can detonate four or more Locust all at once. Quickly ready another arrow, as a Boomer charges the front door with a battering ram.

Chances are, the Boomer will reach the door and create an opening for the other Locust. Fear not; they are easy targets as they funnel through the fiery front door area. Take down as many Locust outside as you can, then rush to the stairs in the foyer and use Frag Grenades and the Lancer to cut down the Drones and Grenadiers that make their way inside.

A second Locust wave launches an attack from the courtyard area. Return to the front window and use the Torquebow to take out the Boomer. Then concentrate on finishing off the Drones. By the time Marcus accomplishes this, Jack will be done downloading the data files. It's time to head for the APC. Go downstairs to the main entryway and pass through the recently opened door to the right of the staircase.

ADAM FENIX'S ESTATE
4 OF 4

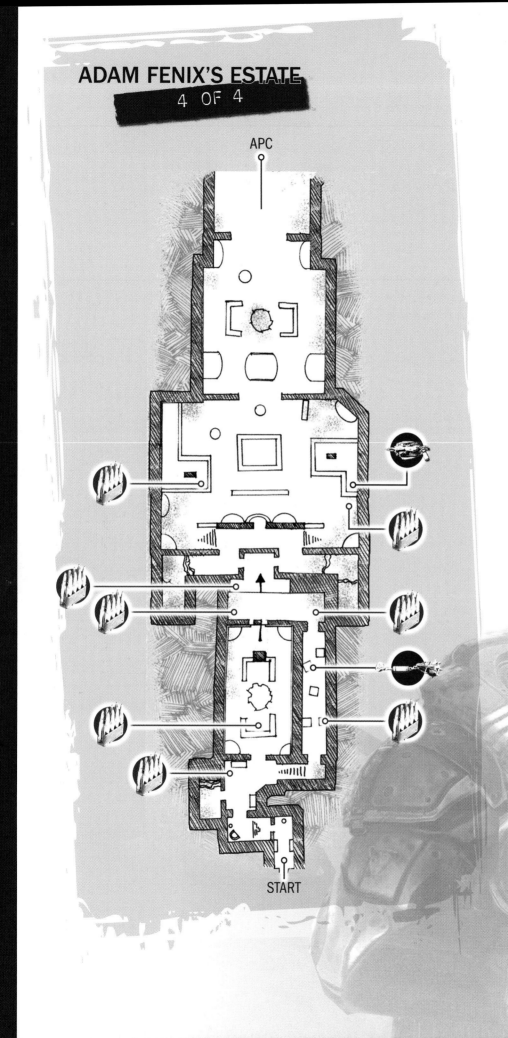

APC

START

ACT 4

THE LONG ROAD HOME

GET TO THE BACK OF THE HOUSE

The door that leads to the rear courtyard is barred shut from the outside—Marcus must unblock it if he's to reach the APC. Ascend the stairs to the right, and proceed through the spider-webbed attic to the hallway overlooking the courtyard.

HIDDEN AMMO!

Use the chainsaw bayonet to break apart the crates and furniture in the attic. Some of these destructible objects conceal Frag Grenades and other ammunition. Check the map for details.

Use a Frag Grenade to close the Emergence Hole in the small courtyard's center. Then finish off the remaining Locust with the Lancer while you have the drop on them. Now it's time to unblock the door at the other end of the yard. Use the Lancer to shoot apart the wooden boards propped against the door. You can also blow them apart by shooting the propane tank to the right of the door.

Return to the previously barred door and proceed through the small interior courtyard to the next hallway. The main backyard is just outside. Take either of the exits and be prepared to make a run for it!

ESCAPE USING THE APC IN THE BACKYARD

Equip the Torquebow and slide into cover along the center of the front wall. This helps ensure that the two Boomers entering the backyard's far end congregate together. Immediately fire on them with the Torquebow. Dom's assistance goes a long way toward drawing some of the Boomshot blasts his way, and it helps kill the Boomers.

GET TO THE APC NOW!

Once the two Boomers are destroyed, a time appears onscreen. Marcus has thirty seconds to cross the remainder of the yard and reach the APC. Don't look for weapons. Don't try to close the Emergence Hole that opens. And don't look for extra ammo. Just run like hell!

ACT 5: DESPERATION

REAVER

These enormous, flying beasts serve as airborne vehicles for the two Locust on their back, one of which usually has access to a Troika! Aim for the Reaver's chest cavity to kill it, or simply shoot and kill its passengers.

ACT

DESPERATION

SITUATION
REPORT

Delta Squad managed to escape the Brumak's wrath by the slimmest of margins and drove without pause to the train station. According to Anya, a train carrying the Lightmass Bomb is due to travel past the station any minute. Delta Squad must somehow board the train in motion and program the Lightmass Bomb with the data retrieved from Adam Fenix's secret laboratory. This may be the only opportunity to inflict the type of damage on the Locust Horde that the humans earlier unleashed upon their own civilization.

TAGS

28
Just inside the doorway that Jack has to rip
open on the fifth train car.

29
On the floor, inside the train car that has
Troikas on its roof.

30
In the small room on the fifth car in Tyro
Pillar's section three.

SPECIAL DELIVERY

Secure the platform and catch the train.

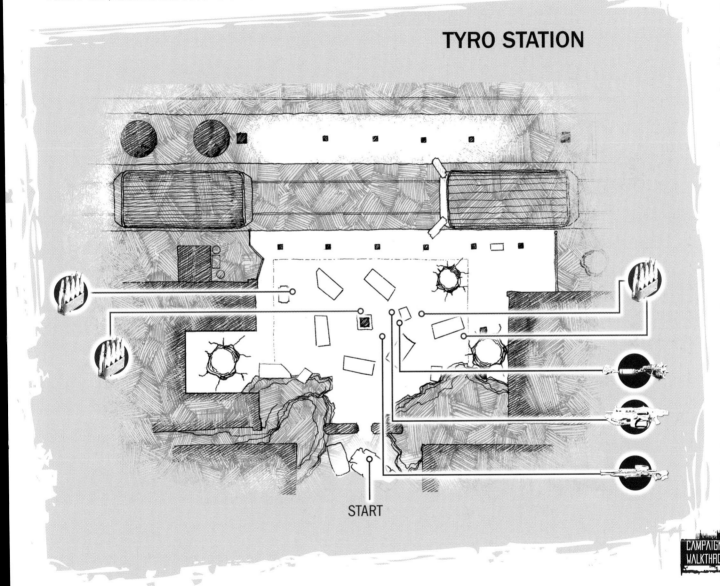

TYRO STATION

START

GET TO THE TRAIN BOARDING PLATFORM

Marcus and the others arrive at the train station only to find that there are numerous Snipers on the roof above the platform. Dom, Baird, and Cole do a very good job of splitting up, taking cover, and shooting down the Snipers. Use the Torquebow to assist the others in eliminating the Snipers—start with the Sniper behind the leftmost piece of cover atop the roof. When he dies, this particular Sniper drops his Longshot down to the ground. Swap out the Torquebow for the Longshot and commence sniping! Your first target should be the Sniper on the roof behind the third barrier from the left.

Wretches start to appear as the last of the Snipers on the platform roof are defeated. Another Sniper appears on a building in the parking lot's corner, near the starting point. Take cover behind a car or the statue and take him out. From time to time, an Emergence Hole opens in the area to the left. Use a Frag Grenade to seal it. This happens at least four times before you hear the sound of the approaching train.

Once the whistle starts blowing, make a run for the boarding platform. Use the wooden planks as a bridge, and cross over the first set of tracks to get in position to board the train known as Tyro Pillar.

TRAIN WRECK

All aboard.

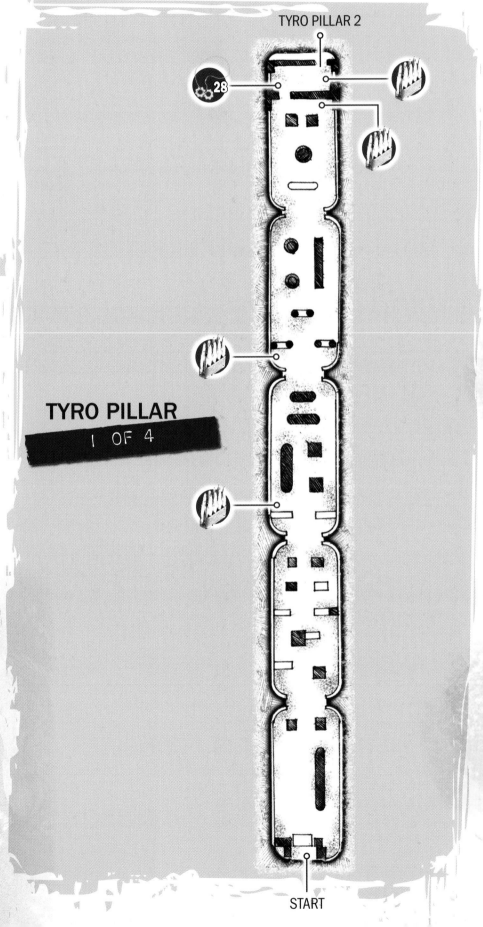

TYRO PILLAR 2

28

TYRO PILLAR
1 OF 4

START

GET NAV DATA TO THE LIGHTMASS BOMB

Baird and Cole are too slow getting to the train, so it's up to Marcus and Dom from this point on! Shoulder the Longshot and begin advancing toward the front of the train. Marcus and Dom find plenty of available cover and should have little trouble progressing past the first few cars. The Drones and Theron Guards are spread out and present easy targets, especially for a skilled marksman.

Advance to the front of the fifth train car. There's no hurry; just use the Longshot and get there safely. Press the button to open the door. Unfortunately, Jack is the only one who can open it. Even worse, a Berserker rapidly approaches Marcus' position from the rear of the train!

ELIMINATE THE BERSERKER THREAT

Thanks to the Nemacysts' ink trails, the sky is too dark to use the Hammer of Dawn. One option is to lure the Berserker to a position next to the flammable gas tank and then detonating it. Marcus can also rid the train of the Berserker by luring the beast back onto the second (or first) train car and then disconnecting it via the coupler on the third car. Carefully bypass the Berserker en route back to the second train car. Get the beast to follow Marcus by revving the chainsaw bayonet or by shooting at it. Once the Berserker is on the second train car, step back to the third car and press the coupler device's button to the left (as viewed while you face the front of the train). The cars disconnect and the Berserker is forever left behind.

MISS THE TRAIN? NO PROBLEM!

Did the Berserker manage to get back onto third car as you disconnected the second? If so, simply stand in front of the rear of the third car and get the Berserker to charge your position. Dive out of the way, and watch as the Berserker stampedes straight off the back of the train and onto the tracks.

COG TAG #28

This COG Tag is immediately inside the door that Jack rips open on the fifth train car. It's to the left, just as you walk in.

Return to the fifth car and enter it. The Reavers are coming and there's quite a bit of train yet to explore, so get moving!

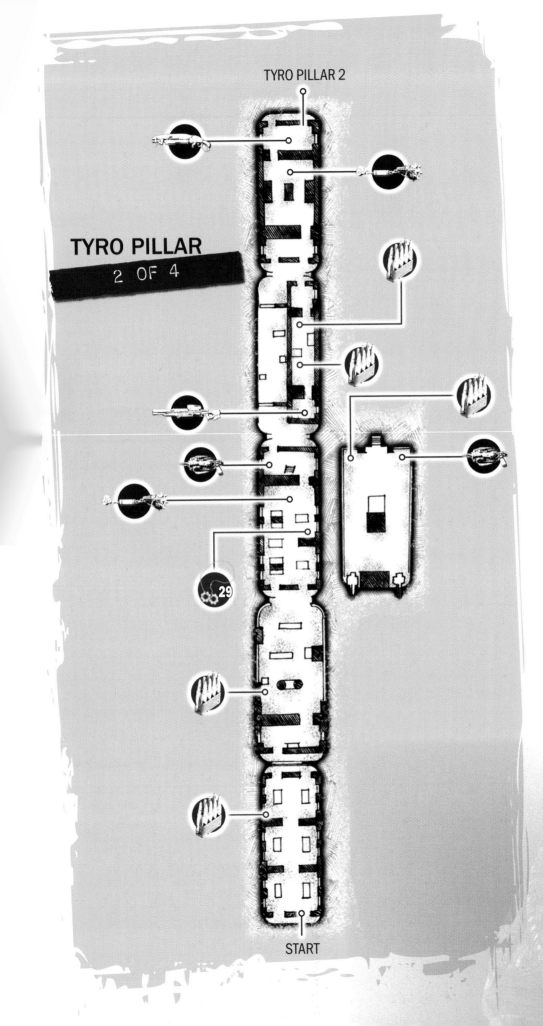

TYRO PILLAR 2

29

START

Now that Marcus and Dom have reached the first set of passenger cars, things are starting to get more claustrophobic. They need to stay away from the windows, as the train is flanked by Reavers. A Troika Gunner and a Theron Guard are this flying beast's common passengers. They're quite deadly if they get within attacking range of Marcus. A few Longshot blasts to the creature's chest cavity is usually all it takes to bring it down.

Use the Lancer to advance past the Drones in the passenger car, and proceed to the next train car. Don't worry about shooting down the Reavers just yet, as more just keep coming. Instead, use the Longshot and Lancer to drop each of the Drones and Theron Guards on the next train car. Then continue inside the far end.

GET TO THE CHAIN GUNS

Anya radios to let Marcus know that this section's third train car has a ladder leading to its roof, where a pair of Troika chain guns is located. Swap out the Longshot for the Torquebow and climb the ladder to the third car's roof to reach the Troikas' location.

COG TAG #29

Before you climb the ladder to the third car's roof, pick up the COG Tag off its floor.

DESTROY THE ATTACKING REAVERS

Grab the extra ammo from the Torquebow on the roof's left corner, and duck for cover behind the cargo crates in the center. Use the Torquebow to take out as many of the eleven Reavers as possible. When you pull back the bowstring, aim at the ground or the crates in order to see the laser sighting, then target the nearest Reaver with it. Don't fire unless the red laser target is visible, else the Reaver is out of range or your aim is off-target. Aim for the Reaver's head or its side.

When you're out of Torquebow arrows, rush to the Troika Gun that's closer to the greatest number of Reavers and fill them full of lead. The Troikas can rotate roughly 160 degrees, so you can't shoot Reavers that advance alongside the train. If one gets that close, either kill it with handheld weaponry or move to the other Troika and wait for it to fall back in line with the others. As you man the Troika, aim for the Reaver's head, and always shoot the one nearest the train first! After you've pasted all the Reavers, return to the lower level and swap out the Torquebow for the Longshot.

KEEP THE TRAIN FROM STOPPING

While Marcus fended off the Reaver onslaught, a large army of Dark Wretches boarded the train. They're trying to stop the locomotive—they obviously know what Marcus has planned! Use the Lancer to down the approaching Dark Wretches, and proceed along the fourth car's left side. Double back through the narrow baggage area on the right. Collect the available ammunition and to kill the lone Dark Wretch near the Longshot in the back. Continue through this section's fifth car to the next area of the train.

CAMPAIGN WALKTHROUGH

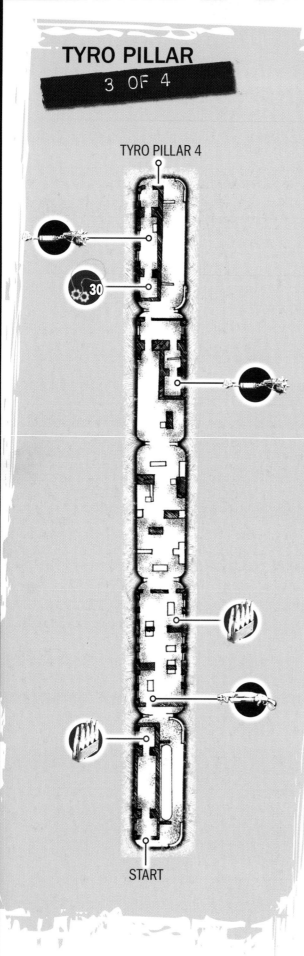

TYRO PILLAR

3 OF 4

TYRO PILLAR 4

30

START

Marcus and Dom are flanked by a pair of Reavers upon reaching this third section of the train. Use the Lancer to gun down the Reavers—it takes roughly 80 rounds per Reaver. Duck in and out of the previous train car for cover when necessary. To advance toward the front of the car, press the button on the car's right side to release the enormous cylinders from the storage rack. This gives Marcus and Dom a way past.

Pick up the Gnasher on the way into the next car and give Dom the "Attack" command right away. Nearly twenty Dark Wretches are about to board this train car, and they're coming from the ventilation in the ceiling and from the windows. Using the Gnasher allows Marcus to get by with less accuracy, which is a good thing because he needs to move constantly during this fight. The Dark Wretches work hard to surround and kill Marcus, so keep your head on a swivel and reload the Gnasher every chance you get. You *do not* want to get caught in the middle of a reload when the Dark Wretches bear down on all sides!

Anya and Hoffman alert Marcus that he has just 45 seconds to make his way to this section's fourth car before the Dark Wretches pull the coupler. Make a run for it! There are several more Dark Wretches on the third car, but the area is rather open and Marcus and Dom can easily shoot their way past the foes as they appear. Get to the fourth car, and then turn around to shoot any remaining Dark Wretches from the safety of your position.

GET NAV DATA TO THE LIGHTMASS BOMB

Grab the Frag Grenades from inside the fourth car and proceed to the fifth car. Release the large steel cylinders from the rack on the right to advance to the far end of the car. Then double back through the interior cabin to collect the final COG Tag in *Gears of War*.

PALE HORSE

Payback.

TYRO PILLAR

4 OF 4

COG TAG #30

The final COG Tag is on the small storage room's floor in the fifth car of the train's third section. Be sure to get it before you advance to the train's next section, as you'll never a second chance.

KILL RAAM

Gather up the Lancer and Longshot ammo in this section's first train car. Continue to the next area. It all comes down to this: Marcus versus RAAM, the Locust Horde's most powerful general. Marcus doesn't have much time, so he must work fast to kill RAAM. Then he must reach the Lightmass Bomb to load it with the Locust network data map.

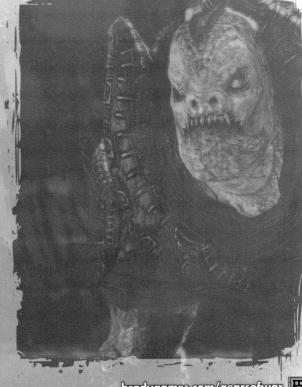

Although Dom and the nearby King Raven chopper help to distract RAAM, this is Marcus' show. If anyone will finish this fight once and for all, it's going to be him. After all, RAAM is the one that killed Marcus' father, Adam.

RAAM begins the fight on this section's third train car. He wastes no time in starting to spray chain gun bullets all over the place. Take cover behind the barrier at the starting point. In addition to his mighty gun, RAAM has a flock of Kryll that surround him like a carnivorous, feathery, protective aura. Marcus cannot harm RAAM as long as the Kryll are nearby.

Fortunately, you can scare the Kryll away from RAAM's side by shooting him at long range with the Torquebow. Watch for the Kryll to scatter, quickly switch to the Lancer, and proceed to empty a clip and a half into him.

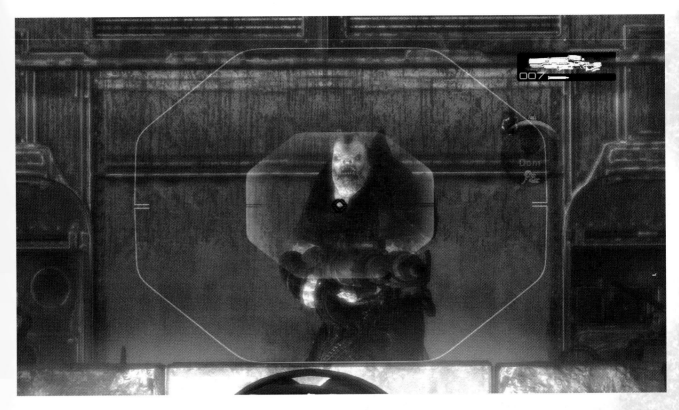

Using this strategy, it should take only a few Active Reloads to finish RAAM. If it takes you a little longer, he gradually marches the length of the train car to attack Marcus from close range. Continue scaring off the Kryll and pumpimg RAAM full of Lancer file as he gets closer. If RAAM gets all the way up to the small barrier, Marcus can inflict heavy damage with Lancer blindfire.

Of course, it's impossible to survive near RAAM for long, thanks to his incredible size and strength, not to mention his chain gun. Wait for him to take a break from firing, quickly hurdle the barrier, and Roadie Run to the identical barrier at the train car's far end. Hop over the barrier, duck into cover, and resume sniping at him in the other direction. The idea is to inflict as much damage as possible from behind cover, right up until RAAM tries to round the barrier and attack at close range. Then run like heck to the other side and repeat!

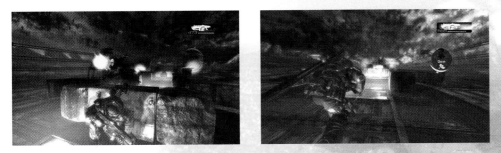

The Locust Horde isn't just going to sit around and watch its leader take damage. Reavers carrying Troika Gunners, Drones, and even the occasional Theron Guard fly into range alongside the train, attempting to kill Marcus while he focuses on RAAM. Fortunately, the boys in King Raven eliminate many of the Reavers, but Marcus must cap them himself if they get a clear shot on him. The best way to do this is to shoulder the Longshot and shoot the Reaver's chest while you're zoomed out.

Swarms of Kryll occasionally show up, making it imperative that Marcus stay in well-lit areas at all times. Unfortunately, this means you can't use the Troika on the third car's platform. Dom and the guys in King Raven do a good job alerting Marcus when the Kryll approach or a Reaver moves into position. It may sound like you have a lot on your hands, but the key to beating RAAM lies partly in keeping away from the Kryll and Reavers. Naturally, RAAM's mighty chain gun is a big threat. As long as you use cover and pick the right moments to dash toward the train car's other end, you should get through in one piece.

12

CAMPAIGN
WALKTHROUGH

CONGRATULATIONS!

You've defeated RAAM and loaded the data to the Lightmass Bomb! Sit back and enjoy the ensuing destruction. After you've viewed the credits and gloated over your newly earned Gamer Points, check out the Options menu and view the credits a second time. Did you know Cole likes to sing?

CO-OP STRATEGY

One of the most engaging aspects of *Gears of War* is the ability to play through the entire campaign with a friend in Co-Op mode. You can do this via Xbox Live, System Link, or even in split-screen on the same television. In Co-Op mode, one player assumes the role of Marcus while the other plays as Dom. Together you must fight your way through the most harrowing 36 hours of these soldiers' lives in a quest to defeat the Locust Horde.

This section of the strategy guide contains tips and tactics specific to Co-Op mode. It's intended as a supplement to the main "Campaign Walkthrough" portion of this book. Although the actual gameplay is the same as when you play alone, there are advantages to partnering with another human player. This chapter's goal is to help you get the most out of your Co-Op experience, especially since we expect many of you will attempt to utilize this feature on the Hardcore or Insane difficulty settings.

ACT 1: ASHES

JACINTO MAXIMUM SECURITY PRISON

RECON

THOSE WHO CHOOSE THE "COMBAT" ROUTE ENTER FROM THE FLOOR ON THE LEFT, WHILE THOSE WHO CHOOSE "TRAINING" DESCEND THE STEPS ON THE RIGHT.

MARCUS AND DOM ENTER TOGETHER THROUGH THE DOOR TO THE RIGHT.

When you enter the lower level of the prison blocks, one player should take cover just outside the side entrance to provide covering fire as the other player flanks along the short walls to the left, past the sealed door. This allows the flanking player to gain position on the Drone behind the wall in the corner.

In the prison yard, direct one player to take cover near the wall outside the door on the right. Meanwhile, the other player moves into position atop the walkway on the left. Once the flanking player gains position on the enemy and draws their attention, the player near the entrance can push forward and flush the enemies out of cover.

EMBRY SQUARE

RECON

DELTA SQUAD CLIMBS THE STEPS TO THE FAR LEFT. ADVANCE BEYOND THE COLUMNS TOWARD THE EMERGENCE HOLE.

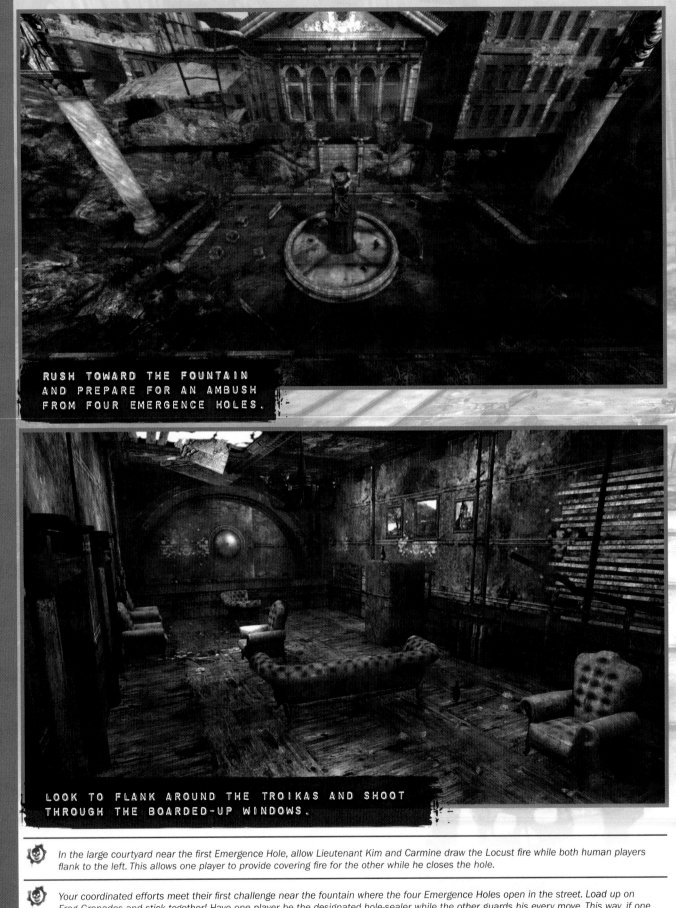

RUSH TOWARD THE FOUNTAIN AND PREPARE FOR AN AMBUSH FROM FOUR EMERGENCE HOLES.

LOOK TO FLANK AROUND THE TROIKAS AND SHOOT THROUGH THE BOARDED-UP WINDOWS.

In the large courtyard near the first Emergence Hole, allow Lieutenant Kim and Carmine draw the Locust fire while both human players flank to the left. This allows one player to provide covering fire for the other while he closes the hole.

Your coordinated efforts meet their first challenge near the fountain where the four Emergence Holes open in the street. Load up on Frag Grenades and stick together! Have one player be the designated hole-sealer while the other guards his every move. This way, if one of you get downed—and chances are, one of you will—the other will be right there to lend a helping hand. Refer to the map in the main "Campaign Walkthrough" chapter to see the Emergence Hole locations.

After rejoining beyond the split path, leave one player in the room with the tile floor while the other flanks to the right, eliminates the Spotter, and takes out the Troika Gunner. By doing so, the player hanging back will already be in perfect position to close the Emergence Hole that opens. However, the other player must quickly get to the Troika and offer support, as several Drones usually reach the surface in time.

RECON

USE THE SANDBAGS FOR COVER AND ENTER THROUGH THE RIGHT-HAND DOOR TO FLANK THE TROIKA.

WHEN LT. KIM LOWERS THE DRAWBRIDGE, DEFEAT THE SEEDER TO REENTER THE BUILDING IN THE FAR RIGHT CORNER.

CO-OP STRATEGY

TAKE COVER ON THE BROKEN BRIDGE WHILE FIGHTING THE SEEDER.

THE HALLWAY ON THE RIGHT PROVIDES A WAY TO BYPASS THE TROIKA GUNNER IN THE DISTANCE.

USE THE TROIKAS ON THE ROOF TO
SECURE THE AREA OUTSIDE THE HOUSE
OF SOVEREIGNS FOR EXTRACTION.

You can tackle the battle on the front steps of the House of Sovereigns by having both Dom and Marcus move through the interior hallway from right to left toward the Emergence Hole. Take cover alongside one another near the hole, and use blindfire and Frag Grenades to squelch the surfacing Drones and Grenadiers. Once you're outside, have one player man the Troika while the other takes cover behind the sandbags to the right. That player can provide crossfire on any Drones that reach the steps.

Your patience and ability to stand back-to-back in the heat of the battle is tested in the hallway where the Wretches appear. Equip the Gnasher and allow the Wretches to advance within a step or two your position, and then shoot from the hip. Both players should first face the lengthier side of the hallway and then turn around later to deal with the Wretches that climb out of the massive hole.

Both players can pick up a Hammer of Dawn inside the first library. Go outside the door and quickly kill the first Seeder with the two Hammers of Dawn. Now have the player with the most Lancer ammunition swap out the Hammer of Dawn for the Gnasher he likely dropped in the library. As for the second Seeder, try to kill it as quickly as possible, trusting that the other player can keep both of you safe from the Wretches that attack on the balcony. For the third Seeder, have the player with the Lancer concentrate on killing Nemacysts and serving as a spotter for the one with the Hammer of Dawn.

After you kill the second Seeder, follow Kim through the door. Have one player step out onto the sanctuary's balcony straight ahead while the others descend the stairs. This gives him the balcony player a perfect vantage point for killing the Drones and Wretches that enter near the altar.

When you attempt to provide cover for Alpha Team from atop the House of Sovereigns, have one player use the Hammer of Dawn against the Drones in the street. The player with the most Lancer ammunition should use it and the Troika to keep the sky clear of Nemacysts.

TOMB OF THE UNKNOWNS

RECON

LEAD THE BERSERKER THROUGH THE HEAVY, "SMASHABLE" DOORS TOWARD THE COURTYARD.

THE WIDE-OPEN SPACE OF THE COURTYARD PROVIDES PLENTY OF ROOM TO MANEUVER AROUND THE BERSERKER.

The best way to exploit two human players against the Berserker is to leap-frog one another in luring her from one door to the next. Have one player set up near a door and attract the Berserker's attention while the other hangs back in one of the Tomb's dark recesses. Once the Berserker opens the door—and while she is still stunned—have the other player slip past her into the next room. Quickly turn and fire to lure her away from the player who initially served as bait. Then move to the next door. Repeat these steps until she's outside, where both of you can use the Hammer of Dawn to kill her quickly.

ACT 2: NIGHTFALL

EPHYRA STREETS

RECON

USE THE CARS AND TREES FOR COVER FROM THE SNIPERS IN THE BUILDING AT THE END OF THE ALLEY.

CO-OP
STRATEGY

BULLETS CAN TRAVEL THROUGH THE CHAINLINK FENCE, WHICH MAKES IT POSSIBLE TO COVER ONE ANOTHER.

When you go inside after the split, allow the player who follows the left route to collect the nearby ammo and Frag Grenades before the other player approaches the balcony and triggers the Boomers' arrival. To deal with the Boomers, have the player on the balcony dive into cover and blind-toss Frag Grenades over the railing.

The two teams emerge from the building on opposite sides of the chainlink fence. The team on the right-hand side must quickly take out the Sniper in the building, and then lend a hand to the teammates on the left. When the left side is cleared, that team should advance under the overhang. This puts them in perfect flanking position for the Locust exodus from the building on the fence's right side. When it's time to take out the Troika, issue the "Attack" command to have Baird and Gus advance on the Troika and flush out the Gunner from behind his post.

On the bridge, both players can push the car toward the Troika. Stick together while one player uses a Frag Grenade to kill the Gunner. This allows you to revive one another if necessary. With the Troika silenced, split up and sweep forward toward the Emergence Hole; one player takes the left side of the street and the other takes the right.

On the ferry, have the player that's not cranking the wheel snipe the fluorescent lighting along the path. Pitting the Kryll against the Drones is especially useful on the harder difficulty settings.

RECON

SHOOT EVERY PROPANE TANK YOU SEE TO
CREATE ENOUGH LIGHT TO WARD OFF THE
KRYLL.

THERE ARE PROPANE TANKS IN EACH AND
EVERY COURTYARD, BUT THEY MAY BE
HIDDEN BEHIND DEBRIS OR FURNITURE.

CO-OP
STRATEGY

ONE PLAYER HAS TO USE THE SPOTLIGHT
TO HELP THE OTHER PROCEED DOWN THE
STREET TO THE LIGHT SWITCH.

THERE'S PLENTY OF LIGHT AT THE GAS STATION,
PROVIDED YOU REMAIN NEAR THE PUMPS, THE
OFFICE, OR IN THE STREET BY THE MEDIAN.

The journey to Chap's Gas Station plays out very similarly in Co-Op mode. Advance cautiously and have one player hold onto the Longshot to take out distant lights located above the enemies. Keep to separate sides of the street and exploit one another's positioning as you detonate the propane tanks. This minimizes the amount of time each of you spends away from cover.

When the battle at the gas station begins, both players should hunker down inside the station's office and ready the Frag Grenades. Toss the Frag Grenades over the median in the street to eliminate as many Drones and Grenadiers as possible during the initial crush. You can snipe the second batch of enemies from a distance as they emerge near the Junker. Lastly, once you defeat the Boomer, move behind the barrier in the middle of the street to snipe the remaining enemies.

VIADUCTS

RECON

THE HIGHWAY LEADING FROM THE GAS STATION TO THE STRANDED IS LITTERED WITH WRECKED CARS AND FRACTURES.

Marcus drives while Dom operates the UV Turret. Remember that shooting the turret stops the Junker. Drive the car slowly to maximize the distance between the Junker and the Kryll at all times—don't inadvertently hurry toward them. Once you locate the Kryll, have Marcus drive away from them, whether it be forward or backward, in order to maintain a gap. Most importantly, heed Chap's reports on the directions from which they're coming.

ALAMO

RECON

As soon as you reach the Stranded, have one player immediately run to the Troika while the other heads through the window inside to close the first Emergence Hole. This player should then gather the Frag Grenades and join his partner. While one player continues to operate the Troika, the other must focus on closing the Emergence Holes and then shift to detonating the leaking gas pipe and dropping the concrete slab. When it's time to destroy the final Boomers in the massive Emergence Hole, make sure both players are safely behind cover near the building, ready to shoot the propane tanks as soon as they are visible.

CO-OP STRATEGY

THE WALKWAY IN THE AREA'S CENTER SERVES AS A GREAT VANTAGE POINT FROM WHICH TO DEFEND THE CAMP.

ACT 3: BELLY OF THE BEAST

IMULSION FACILITY EXTERIOR

RECON

This area's main battle pits Marcus and Dom against an army of Dark Wretches. Backpedal as you circle the area to keep the Dark Wretches in front of you. Remember to roll to the side if any of the Dark Wretches is about to detonate in close proximity.

IGNORE THE FALLING RAIN AND LOOK FOR THE ELEVATOR TO THE BROKEN WINDOW UPSTAIRS NEAR THE ROOF.

IMULSION FACILITY INTERIOR

RECON

DURING THE MINE CAR RIDE, KEEP YOUR HEAD DOWN AND BLINDARE WITH THE LANCER OR HAMMERBURST.

EACH OF THE TWO LARGE DRILLING
PLATFORMS DELIVERS A BOOMER, SO
TAKE COVER.

The fighting within the Lethia Imulsion Facility is rather sparse, but what few battles there are border on chaos due to the Dark Wretches' unpredictable nature. Stay together so that when one of you is downed, the other can do the reviving. Use the Longshot to pick off Drones and Grenadiers from a distance, so that the only enemies to deal with at close range are the Dark Wretches.

IMULSION MINES

RECON

THE FORK IN THE PATH THROUGH THE
MINES REQUIRES DOM AND MARCUS TO
GO IT ALONE FOR A WHILE.

CO-OP
STRATEGY

AS DELTA SQUAD MOVES DEEPER INTO THE MINES, THEY ENCROACH EVER MORE ON THE CORPSER'S HOME.

AS THEY APPROACH THE PUMPING STATION, MARCUS AND DOM SHOULD STICK TO THE LEFT ROUTE AND WATCH EACH OTHER'S BACKS.

The journey to the pumping station is fraught with numerous Dark Wretch battles, but none more than when Dom and Marcus have to split up. Both men immediately face a seemingly endless army of Dark Wretches. Do not advance toward them. Instead, use cover and the Gnasher to put them down as fast as possible. Also, throwing a pair of Frag Grenades ahead of your position helps reduce their numbers. Although you may be tempted to assist your teammate with his battle, it's imperative that you do this only when you're sure that there are no more enemies on your side. Even then, your efforts are likely better spent shooting Dark Wretches off the ceiling to weaken them before they even become a threat. Further ahead, after the paths crisscross, there are opportunities to help one another. Move slowly together, and leapfrog one another's positions to gain flanking opportunities.

At the pumping station, have one player grab the Torquebow while the other utilizes the Longshot. Together, move down the left path and have Frag Grenades ready to throw at the first Theron Guard wave that appears. From that point on, have one player take cover lower on the path while the other remains safely higher. This allows the team to cover more angles and presents fewer places for the Theron Guards to hide. Stay in these positions until the Theron Guards or Grenadiers begin to circle around onto the rocky path. At that point, rush up the ramp to the pumping station and sweep counter-clockwise to the station's back to meet up with Baird on the other side.

Players cannot "bleed out" in single-player or Co-Op modes. However, each player should stay alert and be ready to revive a downed partner. Have Marcus shoot the Corpser's belly while Dom shoots its mouth. This helps take down the foe that much faster.

ACT 4: THE LONG ROAD HOME

EAST BARRICADE ACADEMY

RECON

THE CAMPUS QUAD PROVIDES NUMEROUS PLACES FOR COVER, BUT ALSO CONTAINS NUMEROUS LOCUST THAT ATTACK FROM THREE FRONTS.

WELL-COORDINATED TEAMWORK WILL BE REQUIRED TO NAVIGATE THE STREETS AND BUILDINGS WHILE MARCUS AND DOM ARE SPLIT-UP.

CO-OP STRATEGY

THE MAIN STREET LEADING THROUGH CAMPUS IS HEAVILY GUARDED BY A SNIPER, TROIKA, AND DOZENS OF OTHER LOCUST.

THE LARGE COLUMNS IN THE CONSERVATORY SUPPORT THE GLASS ROOF OVERHEAD.

The initial battle in the campus quad consists of three enemy waves. When the fighting begins, give the "Attack" command to Baird and Cole. Have both human players take to the boarded-up building's stairs inside the wall on the right. This gives you plenty of room to use the Longshot and Torquebow without significant risk. The second enemy wave comes from behind the closed doors near your position. Move down the stairs and have Frag Grenades ready for the Theron Guards and Grenadiers that suddenly emerge. As you finish off the last of these enemies, gradually make your way toward the landing zone to avoid getting caught in the two Boomers' crossfire.

Split up and move from the side yard, and have the player that takes the upper path provide sniping support. Wait for the player on the ground to collect the weapons and ammo drops before you proceed around the corner toward the Seeder. This way, the player on the ground can eliminate the Nemacysts while the player inside the building gets the Hammer of Dawn and takes out the Seeder.

THE WALKWAY ABOVE THE PLANTERS AND GARDEN AREA PROVIDE A
GREAT VANTAGE POINT FOR THE BATTLE DOWN BELOW.

COORDINATE A DISTRACTION TO GAIN A CLEAN SHOT
ON THE PAIR OF TROIKA GUNNERS GUARDING THE
ROAD TO THE FENIX ESTATE.

CO-OP
STRATEGY

The area between the small chapel and the Troika Gunner
demands teamwork. The player in the street down below must
not advance across the street until nearly every enemy is
defeated. This allows the player plenty of time to cut down the
Wretches that attack. It also gives the player in the building
time to snipe the Grenadiers and Drones. Plus, the player
in the building can snipe the distant Troika Gunner from his
vantage point in the building's corner.

On the last stretch along the waterfront that leads to the Fenix
Estate, pick up the Torquebows from the Theron Guards. These
come in handy against the pair of Troikas near the bridge. To
take out the Troikas, have one player act as the bait while the
other uses the Torquebow to take out the Gunner. From that
point on, work together using the Gnasher and the Torquebow
to eliminate the remaining Grenadiers.

FENIX ESTATE

RECON

THE MANSION'S SECOND FLOOR PROVIDES AN EXCELLENT SNIPING POSITION AS YOU DEFEND THE HOME FROM INTRUDERS.

THERE IS A SECRET LABORATORY LOCATED AT THE REAR OF THE WINE CELLAR.

Work together as you climb the steps from the waterfront to the courtyard where Baird and Cole wait for you. Ascend only one flight of stairs at a time. Stay near each other but on opposite sides so you can flank the Boomer and Theron Guards that appear.

As you defend the front of the house, have one of your team draw the enemy fire from the front window where Baird and Cole were. The other player should flank left. There's plenty of ammo and Frag Grenades in the blown-out room to the left. From there, the player can take out numerous Locust with each grenade toss or Torquebow shot. Maintain these positions until the coast is clear. With both human players working together, it's possible to keep the Locust from entering the house.

ACT 5: DESPERATION

TYRO STATION

RECON

USE THE UPTURNED VEHICLES FOR COVER FROM THE SNIPERS, AND LISTEN FOR THE SOUND OF THE APPROACHING TRAIN.

Have one player take the right and the other take the left as you approach the station. Although this puts you farther apart in case you have to revive each other, it allows you to quickly eliminate the Snipers and gain a perfect position to close the Emergence Holes as they open.

CO-OP STRATEGY

TYRO PILLAR

RECON

THE CRATES AND LARGE INDUSTRIAL SPOOLS PROVIDE PLENTY OF COVER FOR MARCUS AND DOM WHILE THEY ADVANCE TO THE FRONT OF THE TRAIN.

THE LIGHTMASS BOMB AT THE FRONT OF THE TRAIN IS DELTA SQUAD'S ULTIMATE GOAL.

Although the scene that involves a dozen Reavers is challenging when you play alone, having both players rush to separate Troikas across the train car's roof is a big advantage. Conserve your Torquebow ammunition—use the Troikas to down each of the Reavers as it appears.

When it's time to fight RAAM, have one player collect as much Longshot ammo as possible while the other does the same for the Torquebow. Stay together throughout the fight. Have the player with the Torquebow use it to scare off the Kryll that surround RAAM. With the Kryll scared away, both players can unload on RAAM with their long-range weaponry. Continue doing this until RAAM approaches your cover. Then hurdle it and Roadie Run side-by-side to the barrier at the other end. Take cover behind it and continue the fight.

ACHIEVEMENTS

Unlike a lot of games out there, the Achievements in Gears of War are all self-explanatory and require no special tricks or super-human feats from the player. Our strategy for acquiring all available Gamer Points is to play through the game once on the Casual difficulty setting and then play through on Hardcore as the host of a Co-Op game. After that, play through again on Co-Op at the Insane difficulty setting. Although completing the game on Insane also rewards you with the Achievements for the lower difficult settings, there is a massive jump in difficulty from Casual to Insane. The intermediate Hardcore mode provides a nice gradation.

As for the mass of Achievements related to Ranked Matches on Xbox Live, each of these comes to you with time. Standard "first to 5" matches seldom take more than 25 minutes, and many players earn up to 10 or more kills in a single match. If you want those Achievements, just keep playing. Your skills will improve and your kill tally will climb ever higher. The Gamer Points will follow. Good luck!

CAMPAIGN

CAMPAIGN ACHIEVEMENTS	PTs.	DESCRIPTION	% OF 1000 GAMER PTs.	NO. OF ACHVs.	% OF 50 ACHVs.
GAME COMPLETION ON CASUAL					
Prison Breakout	10	Complete the Tutorial (on any difficulty)	1%	1	2%
Completed Act 1 on Casual	10	Complete Act 1 on Casual Difficulty	1%	1	2%
Completed Act 2 on Casual	10	Complete Act 2 on Casual Difficulty	1%	1	2%
Completed Act 3 on Casual	10	Complete Act 3 on Casual Difficulty	1%	1	2%
Completed Act 4 on Casual	10	Complete Act 4 on Casual Difficulty	1%	1	2%
Completed Act 5 on Casual	10	Complete Act 5 on Casual Difficulty	1%	1	2%
Mercenary (unlocks Gamer Pic)	10	Complete all Acts on Casual Difficulty	1%	1	2%

CAMPAIGN ACHIEVEMENTS	PTs.	DESCRIPTION	% OF 1000 GAMER PTs.	NO. OF ACHVs.	% OF 50 ACHVs.
GAME COMPLETION ON HARDCORE					
Completed Act 1 on Hardcore	20	Complete Act 1 on Hardcore Difficulty	2%	1	2%
Completed Act 2 on Hardcore	20	Complete Act 2 on Hardcore Difficulty	2%	1	2%
Completed Act 3 on Hardcore	20	Complete Act 3 on Hardcore Difficulty	2%	1	2%
Completed Act 4 on Hardcore	20	Complete Act 4 on Hardcore Difficulty	2%	1	2%
Completed Act 5 on Hardcore	20	Complete Act 5 on Hardcore Difficulty	2%	1	2%
Soldier (unlocks Gamer Pic)	20	Complete all Acts on Hardcore Difficulty	2%	1	2%

CAMPAIGN ACHIEVEMENTS	PTs.	DESCRIPTION	% OF 1000 GAMER PTs.	NO. OF ACHVs.	% OF 50 ACHVs.
GAME COMPLETION ON INSANE					
Completed Act 1 on Insane	30	Complete Act 1 on Insane Difficulty	3%	1	2%
Completed Act 2 on Insane	30	Complete Act 2 on Insane Difficulty	3%	1	2%
Completed Act 3 on Insane	30	Complete Act 3 on Insane Difficulty	3%	1	2%
Completed Act 4 on Insane	30	Complete Act 4 on Insane Difficulty	3%	1	2%
Completed Act 5 on Insane	30	Complete Act 5 on Insane Difficulty	3%	1	2%
Commando (unlocks Gamer Pic)	30	Complete all Acts on Insane Difficulty	3%	1	2%

CAMPAIGN ACHIEVEMENTS	PTs.	DIFF.	DESCRIPTION	% OF 1000 GAMER PTs.	NO. OF ACHVs.	% OF 50 ACHVs.
COG TAGS						
Time to Remember	10	Casual	Recover 10 COG Tags (on any difficulty)	1%	1	2%
Honor Bound	20	Hardcore	Recover 20 COG Tags (on any difficulty)	2%	1	2%
For the Fallen	30	Insane	Recover 30 COG Tags (on any difficulty)	3%	1	2%

CAMPAIGN ACHIEVEMENTS	PTs.	DESCRIPTION	% OF 1000 GAMER PTs.	NO. OF ACHVs.	% OF 50 ACHVs.
KILLING BOSSES					
My Love for You is Like a Truck	30	Defeat a Berserker on Hardcore Difficulty	3%	1	2%
Broken Fingers	30	Defeat a Corpser on Hardcore Difficulty	3%	1	2%
A Dish Best Served Cold	30	Defeat General RAAM on Hardcore Difficulty	3%	1	2%

CO-OP

CO-OP SPECIFIC ACHIEVEMENTS	DIFF.	PTs.	DESCRIPTION	% OF 1000 GAMER PTs.	NO. OF ACHVs.	% OF 50 ACHVs.
Dom-curious	Casual	10	Complete 1 Co-Op chapter as Dominic Santiago on any difficulty	1%	1	2%
Domination	Hardcore	20	Complete 10 chapters as Dominic Santiago on any difficulty	2%	1	2%
I Can't Quit You Dom	Insane	30	Complete all Acts in Co-Op on any difficulty	3%	1	2%
Total Gamer Points		60		6%	3	6%

VERSUS

VERSUS ACHIEVEMENTS	DIFF.	PTs.	DESCRIPTION	% OF 1000 GAMER PTs.	NO. OF ACHVs.	% OF 50 ACHVs.
Don't You Die on Me	Casual	10	Revive 100 teammates in Ranked Matches	1%	1	2%
A Series of Tubes	Hardcore	20	Host 50 complete Ranked Matches	2%	1	2%

VERSUS ACHIEVEMENTS	DIFF.	PTs.	DESCRIPTION	% OF 1000 GAMER PTs.	NO. OF ACHVs.	% OF 50 ACHVs.
WEAPON MASTERY						
Fall Down Go Boom	Casual	20	Kill 100 enemies in Ranked Matches with the Boomshot	1%	1	2%
Pistolero	Hardcore	20	Kill 100 enemies in Ranked Matches with a Pistol	2%	1	2%
The Nuge	Hardcore	20	Kill 100 enemies in Ranked Matches with the Torquebow	2%	1	2%
I Spy With My Little Eye	Hardcore	20	Kill 100 enemies in Ranked Matches with the Longshot	2%	1	2%
Don't Hurt 'Em	Hardcore	20	Kill 100 enemies in Ranked Matches with the Hammer of Dawn	2%	1	2%

VERSUS ACHIEVEMENTS	DIFF.	PTs.	DESCRIPTION	% OF 1000 GAMER PTs.	NO. OF ACHVs.	% OF 50 ACHVs.
HUMILIATION MASTERY						
It's a Massacre	Casual	10	Kill 100 enemies in Ranked Matches with the Chainsaw	1%	1	2%
Curb Appeal	Hardcore	20	Kill 100 enemies in Ranked Matches with the Curb Stomp	2%	1	2%
Capital Punishment	Hardcore	20	Kill 100 enemies in Ranked Matches with an Execution	2%	1	2%
Crackdown	Hardcore	20	Kill 100 enemies in Ranked Matches with Melee	2%	1	2%
Is it a Spider?	Hardcore	30	Kill 100 enemies in Ranked Matches with Grenade Tag	2%	1	2%
The Money Shot	Hardcore	20	Kill 100 enemies in Ranked Matches with a Head Shot	2%	1	2%

VERSUS ACHIEVEMENTS	DIFF.	PTs.	DESCRIPTION	% OF 1000 GAMER PTs.	NO. OF ACHVs.	% OF 50 ACHVs.
VERSUS SUCCESS						
Always Remember Your First	Casual	10	Finish playing a Versus Ranked Match	1%	1	2%
Don't Hate the Player	Casual	10	Finish with the highest points in a Ranked Match	1%	1	2%
Mix it Up	Hardcore	20	Win a Ranked Match in every Versus game type	2%	1	2%
Can't Touch Me	Hardcore	20	Win 10 Ranked Matches without losing a Round	2%	1	2%
Around the World	Insane	30	Win a Ranked Match on every Versus map	3%	1	2%
Seriously... (unlocks Gamer Pic)	Insane	50	Kill 10,000 people in Versus Ranked Match total	5%	1	2%
Total Gamer Points		370		37%	19	38%
Grand Totals		1000		100%	50	100%

MULTIPLAYER

GAMEPLAY MODES

WARZONE

Warzone allows you to play in a competitive, team-based match to the death.

This is the classic multiplayer game in which all players are equal—everyone has equal health, speed, and access to all weapons. Teams compete to eliminate all of the other team's members. Players who are downed may be revived by a teammate, allowed to bleed out, or executed by the opponent. The game ends when one team defeats all of the players on the other team. This is team-based "death match" at its very best.

ASSASSINATION

Assassinate the leader of the enemy team to win the match.

Each team is assigned a leader—either Hoffman (COG) or RAAM (Locust)—and the goal of the game is to kill the other team's leader. One special rule encourages leaders to actively engage in the fighting: players cannot pick up a given weapon type on the map until their team leader has picked up that type, thus "unlocking" them for his team. For example, the leader can drop his Lancer to pick up a Longshot and then drop it to revert to the Lancer. Only then can his teammates pick up the Longshot. If the leader wants to keep the weapon, he can; others can pick it up after the weapon re-spawns (roughly 30 seconds). The same goes for the other weapons on the map—if players want it, they can get it only after their Leader picks up one of the same type. The player on the winning team who kills the opposing leader becomes his team's leader in the following round. The player on the losing team with the most points becomes the new leader of his team.

EXECUTION

Execute your enemies to gain points.

Execution is very similar to Warzone, but it requires all opposing players to be executed, usually at close range. In Execution, a downed player can be either revived by a teammate or left to continue bleeding. The difference here is that once the bleed-out time elapses, the player automatically heals and returns to the fight. This forces the opposing team to leave cover and move in to deliver a coup de grace, whether via the chainsaw bayonet, the curb stomp, or by shooting the downed player at close range. The only exception to this is a head-shot with the Longshot sniper rifle. The team that survives the battle wins the round.

THE TEAMS

COG CHARACTERS

Players can select from a number of different character skins in multiplayer *Gears of War*. All of the characters—both COG and Locust—begin with the same weapons outlay and ammunition stock, so this choice is strictly aesthetic.

MARCUS: A fallen hero provisionally paroled to fight Locust.

DOM: The guy you want on your side when it all hits the fan.

KIM: A by-the-book officer who bleeds in the trenches with his men.

COLE: A former thrashball superstar turned soldier.

BAIRD: Cocky...but smart enough to know how to survive.

CARMINE: Voted "Most Likely to Get Shot" in the Academy.

REMEMBER

LISTEN FOR MOVEMEN

KALONA

HOFFMAN: A senior officer who can still fight with the best of them.

LOCUST

DRONE: Bred in the hollow to be a bloodthirsty fighter.

SNIPER: Trained from birth to destroy coalition troops.

GRENADIER: Thick skin and skull, with a hell of an attitude.

GRENADIER ELITE: Wants one thing: to tear Gears limb from limb.

THERON GUARD: Elite Locust Guard that's cold, calculating, and vicious.

THERON SENTINEL: The best soldier bred in the hollow.

RAAM: A savage and brilliant Locust General.

MULTIPLAYER

MULTIPLAYER BY THE NUMBERS

WEAPON STATISTICS

The weapons undergo subtle stat-tweaking in the transition from the campaign to multiplayer duty. This applies to the weapons power and ammo capacity. The following tables provide specs for each weapon in multiplayer.

Multiplayer Weapons: Ammo Capacity and Damage at Range

WEAPON	MAX AMMO	MAGAZINE SIZE	BASE DAMAGE	SHORT RANGE	MEDIUM RANGE	LONG RANGE
Smoke Grenade	2	1	None	None	None	None
Frag Grenade	2	1	Varies	Varies	Varies	Varies
Lancer	300	60	42	100%	100%	60%
Snub Pistol	48	12	90	100%	100%	60%
Gnasher	24	8	270	275%	175%	50%
Torquebow	6	1	640	100%	100%	60%
Boomshot	2	1	335	100%	100%	60%
Boltok Pistol	12	6	90	100%	100%	60%
Longshot	11	1	350	120%	100%	100%
Hammerburst	300	60	56	100%	100%	60%
Hammer of Dawn	N/A	N/A	Varies	Varies	Varies	Varies

Multiplayer Weapons: Firing Rate and Melee Damage

WEAPON	FIRING RATE	BASE DAMAGE	MELEE
Smoke Grenade	N/A	None	None
Frag Grenade	N/A	Varies	Varies
Lancer	850	42	120%
Snub Pistol	700	90	120%
Gnasher	60	270	300%
Torquebow	60	640	120%
Boomshot	60	335	120%
Boltok Pistol	60	90	120%
Longshot	60	350	120%
Hammerburst	1250	56	120%
Hammer of Dawn	N/A	Varies	Varies

SCORING SYSTEM

In addition to the wealth of information tracked on the Xbox Live Leaderboards, a scoring system evaluates each player's performance from round to round. Use this system to see who is pulling his weight and to help balance the teams for future rounds. Also, these points are used to determine your online Leaderboard and TrueSkill rankings.

Multiplayer Scoring System

ACTION	POINTS	DESCRIPTION
Suicide	-5	Killing yourself while using a Frag Grenade, Boomshot, or Hammer of Dawn.
Causing Damage	1 to 5	This value increases as you continue to damage your enemy.
Reviving Teammate	10	Hurry to a downed player and press the X Button to revive him.
Curb Stomp	10	Stand above a downed enemy and press the X Button to squash his skull.
Knockdown	10	Shoot the player enough to make him drop to his knees, incapacitated.
Execution	10	Killing someone at extremely close range.
Standard Kill	20	Killing an enemy player who is not yet knocked down.
Leader Assassination	20	Eliminating the opposing team's leader in Assassination mode. This is a bonus award.

GENERAL MULTIPLAYER TIPS

 Don't rush an enemy that knows you intend to kill him with the chainsaw bayonet. If you get shot while you rev the chainsaw bayonet, you're forced to lower it. This makes you extremely vulnerable to attack. If you seek a melee brawl, it's best to fire the shotgun or one of the pistols to render the enemy's chainsaw useless. Or, if your foe doesn't have the Lancer equipped, use another weapon, such as the Torquebow, to hit him with it melee-style. Better yet, go for the Frag-tag!

 If you find yourself outnumbered, look for an adequate hiding place and wait for the timer to countdown to a Draw. It might not be the most honorable route, but it just might keep your team in the match. Consider heading back to the spawn point and crouching in a corner, out of sight. If worse comes to worst, at least you'll see your opponent approaching.

 Know your initial destination before the match begins, and practice Roadie Running to that spot so that you don't bump into any obstacles. Bumping into something during a Roadie Run slows your character and can make teammates run into you, thereby giving the opponent a decided advantage in the race to acquire advanced weaponry.

 In Assassination mode, do not run off by yourself as the leader! It's imperative that the leader stay with at least one (and preferably two) teammates at all times. We can't stress this enough.

 Get acquainted with the characters' voices, more specifically, their utterances as they attempt perfect Active Reloads. This is especially beneficial in a one-on-on standoff, as there's nothing better than knowing your opponent's gun just jammed! Rush him for the win!

 Some of the weapons make easily identifiable noises that are audible through much of the battlefield. These weapons, such as the Torquebow and Boomshot, also have very limited ammunition. Try counting silently to yourself each blast you hear from one of these weapons; you may get tipped off when your enemy runs dry.

 The Execution game type encourages players to rush forward and eliminate downed enemies, but don't rush in blindly! Many times, players leave a downed teammate out in the open as bait, waiting for an overzealous opponent to move in for the execution. Don't go in for the kill until you know the coast is clear.

 There are many instances in which it pays to split up the team and send three members straight toward the enemy while the fourth silently flanks the opponent's blind spot. Avoid splitting into pairs, as your opponents might not take the bait and commit knowing two more enemies lurk the battlefield. Plus, it's harder for the opposing team to ignore an advancing threesome, which makes them more likely to call in reinforcements. This presents a great opportunity for the flanking player to deliver mass damage.

 Players who always utilize cover and remember to roll often and erratically survive the longest in multiplayer. There's nothing easier to kill than an enemy who runs in a straight line or stands out in the open.

 Don't steal kills! There's nothing more annoying than working hard to down an enemy and then having one of your own teammates snipe him in the head as you go for the curb stomp. Don't do it unless you agree ahead of time that it's okay.

 If you get tagged with a Frag Grenade, immediately leap toward the nearest enemy player to take him down with you. Similarly, if you attempt to Frag-tag a player (perform a melee attack while holding a Frag Grenade), quickly roll away from him before the grenade explodes, else you'll likely get taken out in the blast. And don't try this attack without warning any nearby teammates.

 Arguably the most important tip of all is to learn the maps and memorize weapon locations. This way, when the HUD indicates that a Torquebow or Longshot has been picked up, you can quickly ascertain where the enemy (or a teammate) is located and react accordingly. Relay this info to your teammates (who may not have noticed) and adapt your tactics.

 Lastly, you must communicate! Your Xbox 360 came with a microphone for a reason—use it! All of the multiplayer games in Gears of War are team-based and, as a result, require cooperation and teamwork to win. A team full of experienced solo players may win for a while, but even a team with average talent that communicates and plans its attacks cooperatively will almost always come out on top.

MULTIPLAYER

THE MAPS

CANALS

SPAWN POINT

(ATOP BRIDGE)

(BELOW)

(ATOP BRIDGE)

(ATOP BRIDGE)

SPAWN POINT

Canals is one of the only multi-level maps that allows players to regularly run below and above one another, thanks to the three bridges that span the canal. The three bridges provide ample sniping opportunities, but those who don't mind getting their feet wet will find the Torquebow as a pleasant reward. This map's elongated design puts a premium on securing either of the Longshot rifles or the Torquebow. Those with a knack for getting in close and surprising an enemy with a critical melee attack may prove superior.

Have one team member rush to the Longshot on the bridge nearest your team's spawn point. From there, the player can snipe or provide cover fire while the other three teammates attempt to obtain the Torquebow under the central bridge.

Decide ahead of time whether your team will make an all-out rush for the Torquebow—which carries the risk of getting sniped from the opposite side—or take a more cautious approach. There are Frag Grenades on the bridge above the Torquebow. If one teammate gets to them first, he or she can use them to hold back the opposition while another team member grabs the Torquebow.

The pillars on the map's edges provide shadowy cover from which to snipe or attempt surprise melee attacks. They are an excellent place to launch last-ditch attacks when you're outnumbered.

CLOCKTOWER

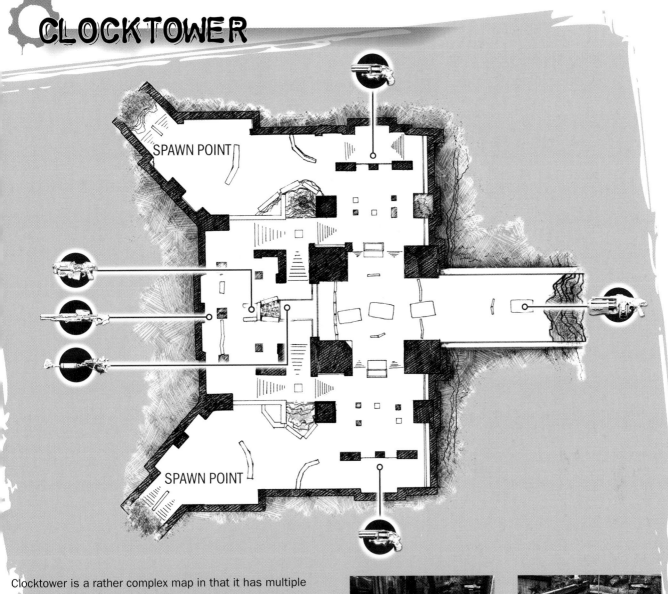

SPAWN POINT

SPAWN POINT

Clocktower is a rather complex map in that it has multiple levels, loads of intricate cover, and a large tower in the center that obscures the view. The map is not as large as some of the others, so there are few places that offer long-range views—much of the action will be up close and personal. Enhancing this element are two dead-end areas that force cornered players to turn and fight. Take it from us; don't try to single-handedly hold off an entire team from the bridge near the Boomshot!

Instruct one member of your team to rush toward the Boomshot location and hide behind the front of the truck. Wait for an enemy to grab the Boomshot, then jump out and surprise him with the Gnasher from pointblank range!

The Longshot location is hotly contested, so sending multiple team members for the weapon is the way to go. This gives you a better chance at acquiring the Longshot. Failing that, it may at least help you counter the enemies' tactics.

Don't overlook the area where the Frag Grenades are located. Many players rush past the area, thus missing out on these desirable weapons. Plus, the position is well covered, making it easier to defend. There's no way to enter the area other than by hopping over the barricades. This little-noticed spot also affords opportunities to jump over the barrier and Frag-tag unsuspecting enemies.

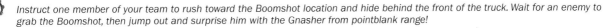

MULTIPLAYER

ESCALATION

SPAWN POINT

SPAWN POINT

In combat, there are few things more deadly than a sniper with an elevated view of the battlefield. Escalation turns this concept on its ear by giving the team at the bottom of this vertical, stair-laden map a pair of Longshot sniper rifles. Meanwhile, the team that starts at the top can only upgrade to the Boltok Pistol and Hammerburst. Can the upper team dodge sniper fire and ambush those at the bottom? Are the players at the bottom skilled enough to pick off enemies at a distance? Your team's talent and organization will certainly be tested one way or the other. Who will ascend to greatness?

The team that starts at the lower spawn point should have two members immediately grab the Longshots and set up a defensive position at the center of the map. Initially, cover is not crucial, as there are no other weapons on the map to match the Longshot's range. Focus your attention on the stairways near the two fountains, as enemies will likely pass those spots.

The players at the lower spawn point who don't get Longshots should grab the Frag Grenades and ascend one level, where they can carpet-bomb the area near the fountains. Obviously, they should stay out of sight and wait until the other team has had enough time to descend.

If you find your team struggling from the higher spawn point, try hanging back to draw out enemies from the lower reaches. Enemies that don't acquire Longshots might be especially tempted to come to you. If you eliminate them, you can then rush the remaining enemies below. Another tactic is to have the entire team pick one path (left or right) and rush the lower area, hoping to massacre the other team's snipers at close-range.

FUEL DEPOT

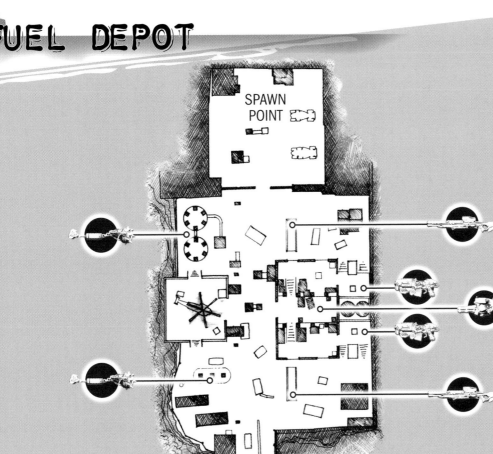

SPAWN POINT

SPAWN POINT

In this spacious outdoor map, teams fight amongst an explosive fueling station, look for weapons in the backs of trailers, and take cover behind a King Raven helicopter. Some will flock to the Hammer of Dawn inside the area's central warehouse, where the stacks of containers and ledges provide ample opportunity to hide. There's little doubt that this map caters to those who don't mind a bit of the ol' run-and-gun, but tactics and strategy—and a well-timed Hammer of Dawn attack—will likely prevail in the end.

The Hammer of Dawn located in the central warehouse can be used from inside as long as the targeting reticule is located outside and within eyeshot. This can be useful for setting up a defensive situation in the warehouse or to blast enemies seeking either of the Longshots in the trucks outside the partially open bay doors.

When the match begins, have two team members rush the Longshot location nearest your spawn point. One can use the Lancer to attack the opposite Longshot location through the partially open bay doors while the other obtains the weapon.

The hangar spawn area can be a good spot to set a trap for the opposing team. Have two members take up positions in the front corners near the entrance, while a third acts as bait by drawing the enemies' attention and then falls back deeper into the hangar.

GRIDLOCK

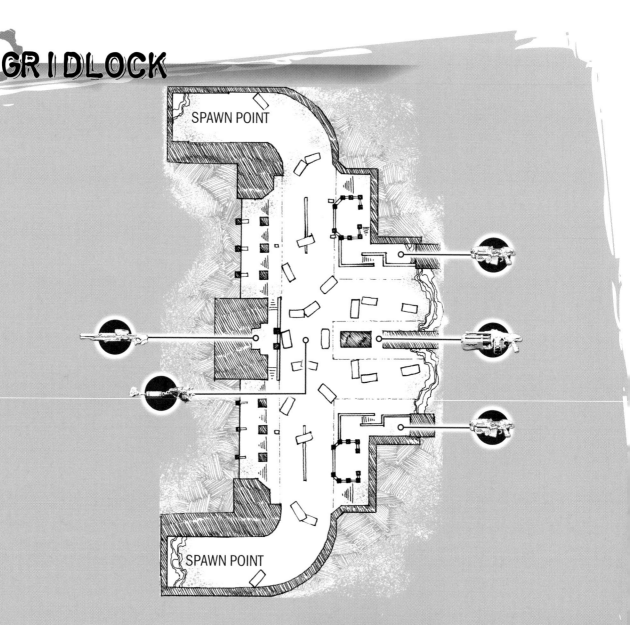

SPAWN POINT

SPAWN POINT

Gridlock is arguably the best map for first-time players to learn multiplayer fundamentals in *Gears of War*. This symmetrical map features just two of the advanced weapons, both equidistant from the spawn points. A number of bombed-out cars and trucks provide plenty of cover, not to mention the two platforms and staircases at the corners. Try hiding in the backs of the pickup trucks for some superb three-sided cover!

If your team manages to secure the Longshot, have your sniper stay at the weapon's location with one partner for defensive support. Snipe from the cover of the balcony while the partner hangs back, out of sight, guarding against enemies that flank the sniping position.

Jumping into the backs of pickup trucks gives you a unique cover location, which players don't normally expect. You can use truck beds to ambush enemies exiting the areas where the Longshot and the Boomshot are located. They're also great hiding places when you're the last man standing on your team.

When you attempt to secure the Boomshot, be aware that enemies could be lurking in several nearby locations: the walls opposite the hall where the Boomshot is located; the nearby trucks; and, perhaps most importantly, the high ground opposite your approach. These spots present danger as you advance toward the Boomshot. Conversely, you may choose to take a defensive stance, wait for an enemy to rush the Boomshot, and have several teammates spring the trap. The combination of a downed teammate and the Boomshot might lure opposing players, giving you a chance to score a second enemy casualty.

MANSION

SPAWN
POINT

SPAWN
POINT

The Mansion is certain to be among the most played maps,
if not for the distinctly different indoor and outdoor areas,
then for the amazing rain effects and breakable furniture.
In Mansion, teams take up arms along several different
fronts: they can wage war in the courtyard, inside on the first
floor, or upstairs on the balcony. The immediate rush to the
Boomshot and Longshot often results in a tense standoff, only to be followed by surprise ambushes and
adrenalin-pumping manhunts.

When you rush for the Longshot, have three team members go upstairs to secure the weapon while one stays downstairs. Have this
fourth player sneak up the staircase and attack any enemies that try to rush from the other side at close range. The crossfire between
the teams upstairs should serve as a distraction.

If your team encounters no resistance seeking the Longshot inside the house, take cover near the front door. Chances are the enemy
will enter from that direction after they gather weapons in the garden area. In the opposite case, if your team finds no resistance in
the garden, try doubling back to the mansion's side entrance near the spawn point. Ambush any enemies who may be targeting the
front entrance.

Any attempt to obtain the Boomshot should not be made alone unless you know that most of the enemy team has entered the
mansion. You can use the Frag Grenades outside the front door to harass the enemy squad while your teammates move in
for the Boomshot.

MAUSOLEUM

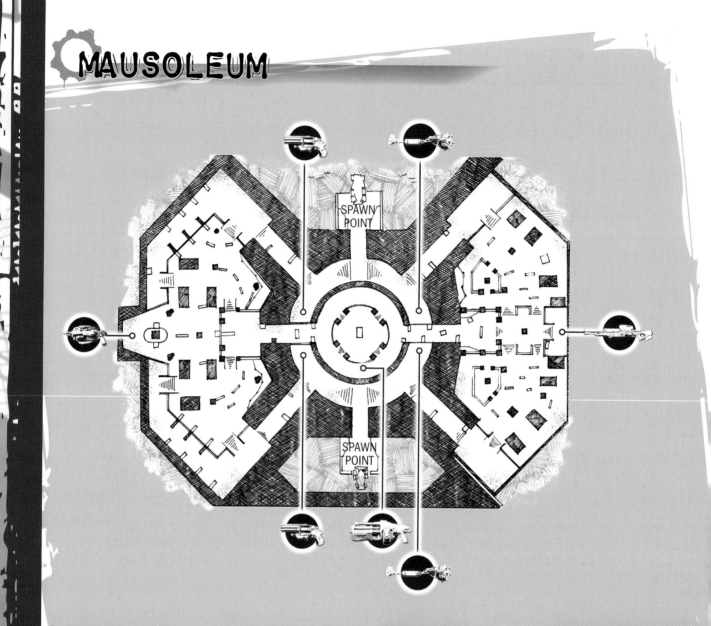

Possibly the largest map, and definitely the most complex, Mausoleum is roughly circular and features distinct "rings" that keep the action tight and focused. Teams begin on opposite sides and make their ways through the offset corridors toward the inner area, where the Boomshot is located. Or they can move to the map's outer reaches to secure the Longshot or Torquebow. The abundance of grave markers and mausoleums provides plenty of cover (and it scares the life out of your opponent).

You'll find Frag Grenades by a wall near your spawn point; the enemy spawn point, along with another set of Frag Grenades, is on the opposite side of this wall. Try grabbing the Grenades nearest your spawn point and quickly tossing one through the gap between the arch and hedges. You might get lucky and kill an enemy lingering at the opposing spawn point.

Have all four teammates move in unison to one of the outer areas, such as near the Longshot or Torquebow. Take cover behind the tall mausoleums. Wait for an enemy to approach, and attack from cover in force. There are many areas where an entire team can take cover just feet from one another. A wandering enemy unit will be easy to bring down.

Due to the sheer size of the map and the many routes that lead through it, communication is vital. It's very easy to get separated from your teammates in Mausoleum. Only an organized and talkative team will succeed in this arena.

ROOFTOPS

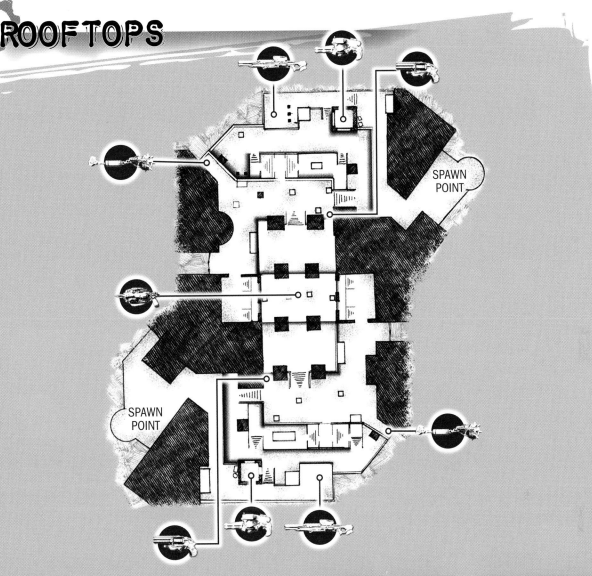

SPAWN POINT

SPAWN POINT

The many elevations, stairs, and side areas on rooftops make for great fun under the moonlit sky. Players can exploit the various elevations to lay traps for their enemies. The small, garage-like rooms on opposite sides of the map make for great foxhole-like places to hide! The Longshot, Torquebow, and Hammer of Dawn make the narrow paths and confined spaces that much more harrowing.

The Hammer of Dawn and Longshot on each side of the map will be in play by the time the two teams reach the central battle area. Players without one of these weapons can use the Gnasher in a surprise rush against foes who have obtained them; you might catch them off guard.

The garages on either side of the Torquebow location are good spots from which to snipe, but they don't provide as much cover as you might think. Keep an eye out for enemies approaching via wall cover on either side, and consider bouncing a Frag Grenade off of the opposing walls to scare off any would-be assassins.

The Hammer of Dawn is handy for attacking enemies behind the many cramped walls on this map. It's also good for flushing them out of cover. Hammer of Dawn wielders should immediately rush to within firing range of the Torquebow location in an attempt to take out any enemies trying to obtain it.

MULTIPLAYER

TYRO STATION

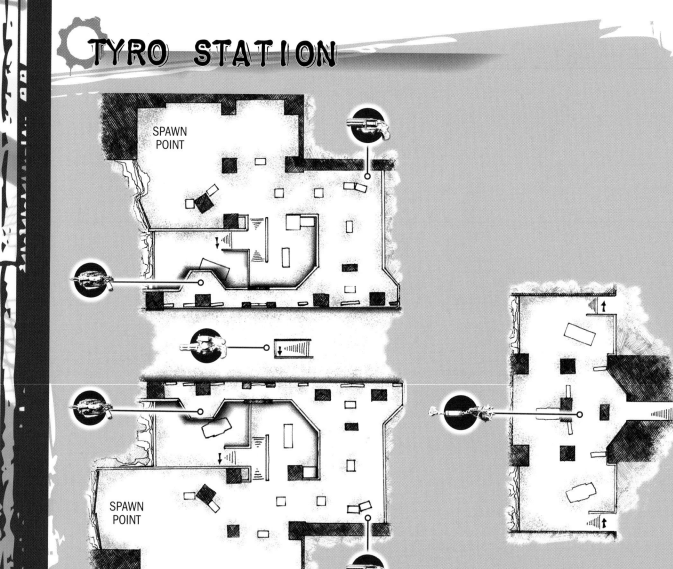

SPAWN POINT

SPAWN POINT

Tyro Station isn't the largest map, nor is it the most complex, but it has one thing none of the other maps has: a train crossing its center every fifteen seconds! Opposing teams often set up front-line stands on their respective boarding platforms. Watch as only the most brave (or foolhardy) try to cross the tracks for a surprise ambush.

Naturally, there's a way to sneak up on your opponents. Use the underground parking lot to slip behind enemy lines and catch them in a crossfire!

The support column nearest the stairs that lead under the tracks provides an excellent point from which to monitor enemy movement in the lower area. Most of the battle takes place in the area near the boarding platforms, but leaving one member here provides an excellent opportunity to guard against enemy flanking maneuvers. It also gives you a decided advantage in that enemies can't see you as they approach. Keep your Gnasher ready!

Don't overlook the Boltok Pistol behind the two dumpsters. It's a powerful upgrade to your sidearm (albeit with a much slower firing rate). You can gain a good angle on enemies across the tracks by advancing from its position to the small sandbag pile near the tracks. Many of the enemies will be focused on your teammates near the Torquebow. Most won't even notice you're there, even after you start firing!

You can use the Hammer of Dawn sitting on the train tracks to great advantage. However, this is by far the most dangerous weapon to obtain. The train that speeds through every fifteen seconds provides a deadly impediment. And, by running out to grab the weapon, you expose yourself to enemy fire from multiple directions. Do not venture out without covering fire, and even then the tactic is not guaranteed to succeed.

WAR MACHINE

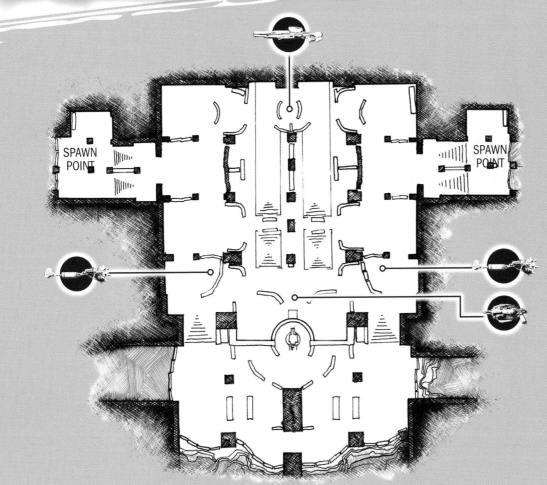

SPAWN POINT

SPAWN POINT

Unlike the other maps, War Machine features a Troika gun emplacement. This is an extremely powerful long-range weapon for the players that claim it. However, it reveals their position and leaves one of their players exposed. The intricate sandbag array provides ample opportunity to take cover, flank, and surprise your enemy, especially because many will be hunkered down, looking for chances to attack from afar with the Longshot or Torquebow.

The Troika in the map's upper area can be very appealing, but it's not as effective as one might think. A team member firing the Troika immediately reveals his position to the enemy, leaving him vulnerable to the Longshot on the map's other side. If you decide to use the Troika, try sitting still until you see a good opportunity to fire, and then quickly move to another area.

There's a Torquebow underneath the Troika and hidden from its reach. Thus, the Troika gunner cannot assault the Torquebow's location. Hence, enemies can flank the Troika via the stairs on either side and use the Torquebow to kill the Troika gunner.

Consider using the Troika as bait. Take cover behind it and set an ambush for any enemies who decide to use it. There are multiple approaches; the best choice is a rear attack, thanks to the Troika's limited rotation. Nothing is more gratifying than a chainsaw bayonet assault from behind, except maybe the always-humiliating Frag-tag. Equip the Frag Grenade and perform a melee attack. Quickly roll away to avoid getting caught in the blast.

DEVELOPER INTERVIEWS

MICHAEL CAPPS
PRESIDENT

What role did you play in the *Gears of War* project?

As President of Epic, my role is to build a great team, give them everything they need to succeed, and get out of their way. The Unreal Engine team and *Unreal Tournament* team also report to me, so I split my time between *Gears* and those other projects.

Give the readers an idea about your day-to-day tasks.

My schedule is extremely variable, because I tend to fill in wherever I'm needed. For *Gears*, I do PR trips, review marketing plans and materials, give feedback on the game design, tweak dialogue scripts, help with scheduling, interface with Microsoft. I manage our relationships for licensed products like the faceplates, strategy guides, and so on. Lately, I've basically been Epic's party planner, trying to find the right date for the gold party, getting people to the release party, that sort of thing. ;)

What was your favorite aspect of the project?

I'm not a 'favorites' 'kind of guy—there's so many things that were fun that I'd never give up. E3 this year was just amazing; we had such a great reception. I love the "Ooooh" I get from a crowd when I pan around one of our environments in a demo, and the cheers I get when I say "this is all real time, we don't do any of that pre-rendered B.S." I guess what I like most is the guys on the team stopping by my office lately saying, "You know what, I played the game through and I freakin' love it! It really is as good as everyone says!"

After they complete the game, what do you expect (or hope) players will say?

I want them to grab their friend, girlfriend, whatever and drag them to the couch so they'll play through it again in co-op.

What was the trickiest task assigned to you and how did you solve it?

A while back, some parts of the gameplay just weren't coming together. It was my unpopular job to say that certain systems needed refactoring, and that others needed cutting entirely. That kind of process can lead to hurt feelings and politics, but I think everyone on the team knew we needed a fresh approach and we came out of it much stronger. People always talk about a game team being a family—and this one really is. Heck, I think we all spent way more time with each other than our families over the past year.

I think I'm the crazy old coot grandfather, who says, "Back in my day, we used Excel sheets for scheduling. And we liked it!"

What did the Unreal Engine 3 allow you to achieve in *Gears of War* that you couldn't have accomplished without it?

All of it!

Despite the advanced Xbox 360 hardware, were there any gameplay elements that just weren't feasible with today's current state of technology?

We pushed the hardware so far with graphics and lighting that we really couldn't go as far as we would have liked with physics. I look forward to more progress in that direction in the future.

What are you most proud of concerning the game?

It passes the mom test for next-generation. That is, even your mom can look at screenshots from this game and say, "Oh, I get it, that's why you want an Xbox 360—your Xbox or PS2 could never do that."

What originally attracted you to the video game industry, and how did you get your start?

I double-majored in creative writing and computer science in college, so I'd always thought about games. Instead, I got my PhD in virtual reality systems and was a teacher. Then one day the Army came along and asked if we could recommend anyone to build a video game for recruiting, and our faculty jumped at the chance. I proposed a squad-based shooter based on latest tech, built a team, and a year and a half later we shipped *America's Army*.

AA was the first game that shipped on Unreal Engine 2—it even came out before *Unreal Tournament 2003* and *Unreal 2*. The Epic guys wanted to start a new studio to build *Unreal* titles, and they tapped me for the job. Scion Studios later merged into Epic, and here I am.

What keeps you in the game industry?

Who knew—it turns out you can meet hot chicks this way!

What titles have you worked on?

America's Army, Unreal Tournament 2003 and 2004, *Unreal Championship 2*, and now *Gears of War*.

Do you have a pet tactic or any tips you'd like to share with our readers?

I'm a pretty good shot, so I play to that. I get into distant cover and aim for the sternum, using the recoil to walk up the body and get a few head-shots in as well. For Raam, it's all about having the Boltok and the Torquebow. I hit him with the bow to clear the Kryll, then pop off six shots into that big head of his. Do that a few times, and it's over.

WHAT'S YOUR...

...Favorite movie?
Just saw *Fearless*, that was cool.

...Favorite food to snack on while gaming?
Sushi. Perfect one-hand food.

...Current gaming obsession (aside from *Gears of War*)?
I don't play video games, I get motion sick. (Kidding!)

...Favorite all-time game?
Unreal Tournament.

...Stranded-on-a-desert-island CD?
And Justice for All.

...Favorite magazine?
Harvard Business Review. Or Playboy.

Favorite book?
White Gold Wielder.

...Hobby?
I love to cook. And eat.

...Secret?
I'm much too snooty for interviews, so I had my secretary handle this.

ROD FERGUSSON
PRODUCER

What role did you play in the *Gears of War* project?

I was the Producer, which means I oversaw development by managing the schedule, setting the priorities, mitigating the risks, and facilitating communication between all of the different disciplines on the team and our publisher.

Give the readers an idea about your day-to-day tasks.

My biggest daily task was to make sure everyone had what they needed to be successful. Usually, that was communicating information between people on the team or to the publisher.

What was your favorite aspect of the project?

My favorite aspect of the project is the "join in progress" co-op play. The ability to be playing *Gears* in single-player and see a friend come online, invite him to join and have him take over Dom without ever leaving your single-player game is awesome. Co-op has always been my favorite feature in any game, and I'm so excited about how we did it in *Gears*.

After they complete the game, what do you expect (or hope) players will say?

I hope they'll say, "That was awesome. Now let's play co-op on Insane."

What was the trickiest task assigned to you and how did you solve it?

Everything about making AAA games is tricky. Hopefully you liked our solution.

What did the Unreal Engine 3 allow you to achieve in *Gears of War* that you couldn't have accomplished without it?

Shipping a game this big with a team this small.

Despite the advanced Xbox 360 hardware, were there any gameplay elements that just weren't feasible with today's current state of technology?

No.

What are you most proud of concerning the game?

I could probably write for pages on all the things I'm proud about, including the team, the process, and the final product. But if I were to pick one small area that I was involved in, I'm especially proud of the voiceover work. I was involved in the casting, the directing, and even some of the writing, and I helped design the combat chatter system. Hearing our very talented cast bring our characters to life and make the game experience that much more rewarding to the players makes me very proud.

What originally attracted you to the video game industry, and how did you get your start?

Being a gamer is what attracted me to the industry initially. When your career is based on your favorite thing to do, how could it be any better?

My path to games was a bit convoluted. I was self-employed as a business analyst doing government database systems when I got hired into Microsoft Consulting Services in Ottawa, ON Canada. As a Microsoft employee, I then decided that my goal was to work my way onto main campus in Redmond and get into the games group. A year and a half later, I had a job offer from Redmond as part of Enterprise Services, and a year and a half after that I was interviewing for *Flight Sim*. Oddly enough, the same day as my interview for the scenery Producer for *Flight Sim*, a new position opened up as the Producer for *MS Train Sim*. I jumped at the chance to produce my own game and got the job.

Twelve years ago, I was doing data flow diagrams for government lawyers; today, I shoot monsters in the face with a shotgun. Nice career path...

What keeps you in the game industry?

First, it's the people. I love nothing more than to be working with passionate and creative people who all love what they do. That's very difficult to find in a typical corporate environment, but not so

for most people working in games. Making games sounds like an easy job but it's not and you really have to want to work on games to keep up with the time and effort required.

Second, it's the work. I've never had a job where I got to do so many fun and creative things. For example, I get to work with the writers to help create dialogue and story, with the designers to help create new ideas and features, with the artists to help shape environments and characters, and with the overall team to determine how we're going to go from nothing to what we hope is an amazing experience. How could you leave that?

What titles have you worked on?

I've worked on several titles that have never seen the light of day—one of which included a focus-group member looking directly at the one-way mirror, saying, "Do not make this game."

In terms of shipping titles, I've worked on *MS Train Simulator* (don't laugh; it sold over a million units worldwide), *Blood Wake* (okay, now you can laugh, but it was fun and I still think *BW2* would have been awesome), and *Counter-Strike Xbox*. If you listen closely while playing *CSX*, you'll hear me as one of the 'bot voices.

What can we look forward to in the future with the *Gears of War* franchise?

It's up to gamers whether the *Gears of War* franchise has a future. But if it does, I'm sure it will be a fun one.

Do you have a pet tactic or any tips you'd like to share with our readers?

So many to choose from... There's the DBNO bait, the suicide hug, the Torquebow mine... Hmmm... Well, I guess one of my favorite tactics is really more about flair than skill. When you get caught out in the open and need to close the distance between you and your victims/attackers, I like to have my shotgun equipped and evade into them. This way, you close the distance fast, make yourself harder to hit, and then, as you unroll, you take off their head with a shotgun blast. When you perform it smoothly, it feels oh so good and a little sticky.

...Favorite movie?

The Fifth Element.

...Favorite food to snack on while gaming?

Diet Mountain Dew to keep up the pace. Who needs all that sugar with their caffeine?

...Current gaming obsession (aside from *Gears of War*)?

The Alpha of the *Burning Crusade* expansion for *World of Warcraft*.

...Favorite all-time game?

No such thing for me. But fondest memories include *Tribes* and *Diablo II*.

...Stranded-on-a-desert-island CD?

"How to Survive While Stranded on a Desert Island" book on CD

...Favorite magazine?

Don't really have one that I read every month. In terms of graphic novels, though, I've been really enjoying *Powers*.

...Favorite book?

Princess Bride by William Goldman

...Hobby?

Playing Poker. Badly.

...Secret?

I only pretend to be Canadian so that I can get all the girls with the cool English accent.

CLIFF BLESZINSKI — LEAD DESIGNER

What role did you play in the *Gears of War* project?

My position is Lead Designer.

Give the readers an idea about your day-to-day tasks.

Brainstorm. Play the game. Harvest, filter, and mediate team member ideas. Write documentation. Engage in many, many meetings. Sell my ideas to the other developers, the leads on the project, the press, management, and ultimately gamers.

What was your favorite aspect of the project?

I'm very happy with many aspects of the game but, in particular, I'm most excited about what Active Reload does for the shooter genre. I can't play another shooter now without wanting to reload faster. I still mess up my occasional AR, which results in a horrid gun jamming for which I blame myself for trying!

After they complete the game, what do you expect (or hope) players will say?

Nothing. I hope they'll take a nap because the game is a beautiful, exhausting experience. So maybe they'll snore a bit.

What was the trickiest task assigned to you and how did you solve it?

Making it fun and useful to employ cover in combat. We used a combination of things, from making the initial decision to slam into cover (with proper audio and effects) to the context-sensitive A Button system.

What did the Unreal Engine 3 allow you to achieve in *Gears of War* that you couldn't have accomplished without it?

Rapid prototyping and amazing visuals are the two main things that come to mind.

Despite the advanced Xbox 360 hardware, were there any gameplay elements that just weren't feasible with today's current state of technology?

I'm not certain there's any gameplay element that a determined designer and programming team could not pull off given enough time and resources. We set out to make a great cinematic cover shooter, and the Xbox 360 happened to be a perfect match for the vision.

What are you most proud of concerning the game?

I'm most proud of the interesting universe we've crafted and the crisp gameplay contained within. For me, the game just "feels" right, and that feel is one of the hardest things to achieve as a designer

What originally attracted you to the video game industry, and how did you get your start?

I knew the moment I played my first game at the age of six that this was the future of entertainment. How could one not find this compelling and want to work in this sector of the entertainment industry?

What keeps you in the game industry?

A desire to see this medium reach its full potential as a commercial and artistic product.

What titles have you worked on?

The videogame series that I've worked on include *Jazz Jackrabbit*, *Unreal*, *Unreal Tournament*, and now *Gears*.

What can we look forward to in the future with the *Gears of War* franchise?

We're not committing at this point to any follow-up products. If we were to consider it, I'd imagine more great combat, visuals, and characterization.

Do you have a pet tactic or any tips you'd like to share with our readers?

Practice with grenades, head-shots, and blindfiring. They'll save your life more often than you'll think!

WHAT'S YOUR...

...Favorite movie?

The Big Lebowski.

...Favorite food to snack on while gaming?

White Rabbit.

...Current gaming obsession (aside from *Gears of War*)?

Xbox Live Arcade.

...Favorite all-time game?

Tetris.

...Stranded-on-a-desert-island CD?

Shiny Toy Guns.

...Favorite magazine?

Ranger Rick.

...Favorite book?

Choke.

...Hobby?

Beer and Travel. In either order.

...Secret?

This is not my real hair color.

LEE PERRY

LEAD LEVEL DESIGNER

What role did you play in the *Gears of War* project?

Lead the design and implementation of the environments through the game, set up combat scenarios, worked with LDs to generate the level geometry, scripting, and audio. Basically, working with LDs to create the game world. Also, loads of boss combat, weapon function, mini-game, and gameplay prototyping.

Give the readers an idea about your day-to-day tasks.

This changes greatly throughout the course of a project. Early on, the tasks involve groundwork design and development. Later in the project, the load shifts to oversight and management of the team, and making decisions about the work that's being done. Lots of meetings, lots of email.

What was your favorite aspect of the project?

Seeing the various approaches to game systems come online and eventually shape something we all found really fun to play. It was also great working with the scripting tools to get much of the early design in a playable form before people had to spend real time on implementing the ideas.

After they complete the game, what do you expect (or hope) players will say?

"Dude! Lets get online!"

Well, and I hope they walk away missing our core gameplay in future games. I want them to play a run-of-the-mill shooter after *Gears* and think, "Wow, it's pretty stupid to be running around in the open like this..." That would be a marked evolutionary step in shooters across the board.

What was the trickiest task assigned to you and how did you solve it?

Probably getting everything in the game to load off disk in a streaming manner and within memory. The levels were blocked in and underway when the decision to make them stream was made. So, we had to retrofit levels to make that happen, as well as adjust all the action, scripting, and ever-evolving gameplay to work with those layouts. However, doing this after the levels were laid out helped make the environments not seem as contrived, or "door-hallway-door-hallway" in layout.

What did the Unreal Engine 3 allow you to achieve in *Gears of War* that you couldn't have accomplished without it?

The tech has been fantastic! The tools were instrumental in allowing us to design and implement gameplay scenarios without having programmers shoulder that load. If we wanted a complex series of events to happen, we could do it as designers and see it working before we ever had to commit to it. It represented a fundamental change in how we designed things. Before, we would have designed so many theoretically fun scenarios on paper; with these tools, we could just try it to see how it works and iterate on the results.

Despite the advanced Xbox 360 hardware, were there any gameplay elements that just weren't feasible with today's current state of technology?

Not particularly. I know it's a great tagline to say we're pushing the 360 as far as it can go, but the reality is that there is a huge space for improvement. By the end of the project, we find that we could easily push substantially more detail than we are in some areas. I grin from ear to ear when I think of what we'll be doing that really will be pushing it as far as it can go.

What are you most proud of concerning the game?

The core gameplay loop. I think we really got something there. It's difficult to ask or expect players to adapt to a different style of gameplay than what they're used to... You really have to offer something spectacular as incentive to relearn how you should play a shooter. We were massively nervous about this through much of production, but once we had it in place and saw that people really were able to pick it up and adapt after only a level worth of exposure, the tension was released greatly—you could hear the sighs of relief from the East Coast to Seattle.

What originally attracted you to the video game industry, and how did you get your start?

I've always wanted to be a game designer—nothing else has ever been on my radar. I started my career as an artist, knowing that people simply aren't looking to hire someone to design a project... You have to work your way into it from another angle. Back in the early '90s, virtually nobody was doing 3D work, but I picked it up as a skill and found myself a slingshot into the industry. More than a decade later, I'm finally getting where I want to be.

What keeps you in the game industry?

The work environment, the creative outlet, the chance to do what I love and support my family with something I'm passionate about.

What titles have you worked on?

UT2003, *UT2004*, *Anachronox*, R&D and cinematic projects at Squaresoft, a fistful of PlayStation and PS2 games.

What can we look forward to in the future with the *Gears of War* franchise?

More than you'll expect. We got the core down, now it's time to have some fun! ←

Do you have a pet tactic or any tips you'd like to share with our readers?

FLANK! This is the one game you're likely to play where it actually counts for something. You can stay behind cover and play whack-a-mole for 10 minutes with a given enemy, or look around for a second and discover there's almost always a side route to make his cover useless...and this goes triple for multiplayer. Don't get sucked in—get behind that sucka!

WHAT'S YOUR...

...Favorite movie?

Conan, *Aliens*, *Better off Dead*, *Matrix*...no, I refuse to answer!

...Favorite food to snack on while gaming?

I'm partial to chocolate-covered sunflower seeds, actually—try 'em!

...Current gaming obsession (aside from *Gears of War*)?

Oblivion caught me for a long time...so fun.

...Favorite all-time game?

Ouch! Um... *Puzzle Fighter*? *Cyberball*? *Shadow of the Collosus*? *Carnage Heart*? *Kings Quest 3*? Can any real gamer answer these? ←

...Stranded-on-a-desert-island CD?

Bob Marley and a hammock—FTW!

...Favorite book?

Game of Thrones currently.

...Hobby?

Woodworking and crashing RC planes.

...Secret?

Watch the credits.

JEREMIAH O'FLAHERTY

What role did you play in the *Gears of War* project?

I was the Art Director on *Gears of War*.

Give the readers an idea about your day-to-day tasks.

Day-to-day is crazy for the Art Director. I tend to get into the office pretty early (i.e. 5-8 a.m. depending on crunch or not) so that I can take care of emails, feedback, cinematic work, and any tasks that require uninterrupted focus. By 10 a.m., many other folks are beginning to arrive at the office and I start working with specific people to give them the direct feedback they need, looking over their shoulder, or us reviewing it on my computer, etc. My role is very much about the beginning (the concepts) and the end (all the pieces coming together), so depending on the stage of the project, I spend more time focused on one or the other. Organized meetings are a huge part of the daily "core hours" time spent. We have Leads meetings, animation meetings, UI meetings, level meetings, monster meetings, etc. Staying on the same page is super important and so is participation in the way things are done, so meetings are a fast way to facilitate those things. Between meetings, I manage emails and walk around talking to other folks on the team about what they are working on.

What was your favorite aspect of the project?

Working on a new franchise with the expectations of *Gears* has been a blast. From the very early days, the *Gears* team has been striving to create a really fun and visually amazing experience, and maintaining that throughout the development has been the goal. From the animation system, to the post-processing, to the cinematics, we tried to push well beyond where we had been before and make something people will really have a good time playing and viewing.

After they complete the game, what do you expect (or hope) players will say?

That it really looks like you are playing in a "movie" environment.

What was the trickiest task assigned to you and how did you solve it?

In general: Working with Cliff to bring his crazy ideas to solid form in the game was tricky at times. I trust his design sense but there are a lot of bad ways to make a chainsaw on a gun, for example. Taking the time to iterate with the concept artist until we believed in the idea as much as Cliff meant we had found a solution.

Keeping the HUD in *Gears* as simple as it is was an exercise in persistence. There are only so many ways to indicate things to the player, and most games depend on color in the HUD to do that. By limiting the gameplay guys to only using black, white, and red, we had to be really creative to make sure the player gets the necessary feedback without betraying the minimalist HUD design.

What did the Unreal Engine 3 allow you to achieve in *Gears of War* that you couldn't have accomplished without it?

It allowed us to make the game look like a feature film. From the subtleties in the shaders, to the lighting, to the post-processing, the engine allowed us to really tailor the look around the filmic style we had set out to create from the very beginning.

What are you most proud of concerning the game?

The overall look and feel turned out great in *Gears*. We achieved a cinematic style in the visual quality, filtering, and motion. The in-game, hand-held camera look of *Gears* that carries through to the cinematics really helps underline that film look that we were after. Add to the fundamental art of the game the weighty feeling of the animations and the physics-blended motion, and we were able to create and finally layer on the coolest blood and gore that I've ever seen pushed into a game. The visuals from top to bottom make me smile with joy every time I play the game.

What originally attracted you to the video game industry, and how did you get your start?

As a blend of technical, art, and film, the game industry has worked out really well for me. When I was twelve, I was programming and designing my own games on the first home computers that came on the market back in the '80s. As computers progressed, my brothers and I would split up the tasks of programming and art, and I gravitated toward the art side of things. At eighteen, the first game for which I had helped design and create the art was published for the Amiga. While continuing to create games full-time, I also went to art school and film school to bone up on some of the fundamentals that I have continued to use to this day. I started making games because it was fun and challenged me in all the right ways. I continue to make games because, after 18 years, it still continues to challenge me and keep me on my toes visually and technically.

What keeps you in the game industry?

The women! Seriously, a wife and daughter with expensive taste. What? Were you thinking I meant "women" like a guy in a band would say it?

What titles have you worked on?

More interesting are the companies I've worked for. I was one of the founders of Ion Storm. I did two years in the desert working at Westwood, and now I'm working at the best game company in the industry. Along the way, I worked on a bunch of Amiga titles, PC titles, and a few console titles.

What can we look forward to in the future with the *Gears of War* franchise?

Oooh. If I told you, then it wouldn't be as much fun to watch the forums (http://forums.epicgames.com) and see what people are guessing.

Do you have a pet tactic or any tips you'd like to share with our readers?

Use cover and curb-stomp as often as you can. We put the gore in there for a reason, so have fun watching your character's skull get crushed and have fun crushing a few yourself.

WHAT'S YOUR...

...Favorite movie?

Right now, Guy Ritchie's *Snatch*.

...Favorite food to snack on while gaming?

Chocolate Chips straight out of the bag.

...Current gaming obsession (aside from *Gears of War*)?

With our focus on making sure we get *Gears* into the hands of gamers as soon as possible, I haven't had anything but this project on my mind.

...Favorite all-time game?

Looks to be *Gears of War* (formerly *Unreal Championship* 2).

...Stranded-on-a-desert-island CD?

What, no MP3 players allowed? Beatles *Sgt. Pepper's*.

...Favorite magazine?

Rolling Stone.

...Favorite book?

Slaughterhouse 5.

...Hobby?

Oil Painting

...Secret?

I killed a man in Reno just to watch him die.

CHRIS PERNA

LEAD ARTIST

What role did you play in the *Gears of War* project?

Lead Artist. This included managing anywhere from 10 to upwards of 20 artists at certain points throughout the project. Interfacing with an art director, producer, designer, engine programmers, gameplay programmers, and level designers on a regular basis to make sure everything runs like clockwork. I was also responsible for a great deal of artwork, lighting, and visual prototyping for the project.

Give the readers an idea about your day-to-day tasks.

Keeping the art team motivated and inspired so that they continuously churned out top-quality work within strict scheduling deadlines was a top priority.

On top of that, I had to keep up with the insane pace set by the artists by creating artwork myself. Outside of meetings and scheduling concerns, my main tasks were character and monster skins, some weapon materials, environment models, materials and textures, lighting levels, and the visual prototyping of certain areas throughout the game.

What was your favorite aspect of the project?

I'd have to say it was getting to interact with such a talented team on a daily basis. It was truly a pleasure to work with the entire team from art to engine, level design to gameplay programming and design.

After they complete the game, what do you expect (or hope) players will say?

"WOW."

I really hope that they have a fun little escape from the daily grind. As an artist, I'd love to hear people saying how nice the game looks, but I also want them to enjoy the whole experience. Gameplay design and sound is also top-notch, and I really hope that people get into the story as well, because it's outstanding.

What was the trickiest task assigned to you and how did you solve it?

Getting a massive amount of content complete without sacrificing quality was probably the trickiest thing for art. We solved this by outsourcing some content, but most of it was a labor of love for the artists on the project, so long hours and extremely talented professionals in-house did an outstanding job.

What did the Unreal Engine 3 allow you to achieve in *Gears of War* that you couldn't have accomplished without it?

UE3 allowed us to push the graphics envelope further than ever before. The sheer amount of polygons on screen is mind-blowing, as well as the texture resolutions, shader complexity, and animation.

Despite the advanced Xbox 360 hardware, were there any gameplay elements that just weren't feasible with today's current state of technology?

Not that I'm aware of. Graphics and AI will continue to evolve as we get more familiar with the hardware, but I think we're pretty satisfied with what we have.

What are you most proud of concerning the game?

I think, for me, it's the overall visual style of the game. It's brutal and raw—everything in the world feels heavy, as if there's mass or weight to it.

What originally attracted you to the video game industry, and how did you get your start?

I started drawing monsters when I was very young (like, two years old). Growing up, that's all I wanted to do. My teachers told me I'd never make a living doing that. I listened for a while and did a few years in advertising and graphic design. Eventually, I started seeing games coming out with cooler and cooler graphics and decided to give it a shot. That was around 10 years ago and I haven't looked back.

It was games or movie effects, and games were easier to get into.

What keeps you in the game industry?

I'm still that little kid who wants to draw monsters and this is where I can do it and bring them to life.

What titles have you worked on?

Lots. *Unreal Tournament 2003* and *2004*, *Anachronox*, *Deus Ex*, *Daikatana*, and now *Gears of War*.

What can we look forward to in the future with the *Gears of War* franchise?

Fun, fun, fun.

Do you have a pet tactic or any tips you'd like to share with our readers?

When in doubt, smash it with a bat.

WHAT'S YOUR...

...Favorite movie?
Alien.

...Favorite food to snack on while gaming?
I don't snack while gaming, too many crumbs.

...Current gaming obsession (aside from *Gears of War*)?
Star Wars Lego 2.

...Favorite all-time game?
Diablo II.

...Stranded-on-a-desert-island CD?
Anything by Slayer.

...Favorite magazine?
Fangoria.

...Favorite book?
Brian Lumley's *Necroscope.*

...Hobby?
Sculpting.

...Secret?
Wouldn't be a secret...

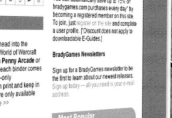

GEARS of WAR

Written by Doug Walsh

© 2006 DK Publishing, a division of Penguin Group (USA), Inc.

BradyGAMES® is a registered trademark of DK Publishing, Inc.

BradyGAMES® Publishing

An Imprint of DK Publishing, Inc.

800 East 96th Street, Third Floor

Indianapolis, Indiana 46240

ISBN: 0-7440-0836-0

Printing Code: The rightmost double-digit number is the year of the book's printing; the rightmost single-digit number is the number of the book's printing. For example, 06-1 shows that the first printing of the book occurred in 2006.

09 08 07 06   4 3 2 1

Manufactured in the United States of America.

CREDITS

Title Manager	Book Designer
Tim Fitzpatrick	**Doug Wilkins**
Screenshot Editor	Production Designer
Michael Owen	**Tracy Wehmeyer**

BRADYGAMES STAFF

Publisher	Creative Director
David Waybright	**Robin Lasek**
Editor-In-Chief	Director of Marketing
H. Leigh Davis	**Steve Escalante**
Licensing Manager	Team Coordinator
Mike Degler	**Stacey Beheler**

ACKNOWLEDGMENTS

BradyGAMES sincerely thanks everyone at Epic for an incredible game, for the butt-kicking maps in this guide, for the gorgeous art book, and for such gracious, professional support. Special thanks to Michael V. Capps, Rod Fergusson, Cliff Bleszinski, Jerry O'Flaherty, Chris Perna, Chris Bartlett, Shane Smith, Mark Rein, Lee Perry, Dave Nash, Grayson Edge, Dave Ewing, Andrew Bains, Sidney Rauchberger, Stu Fitzsimmons, Ryan Brucks, Phil Cole, Warren Marshall, Paul Mader, Dave Spalinski, and Ken Spencer—this guide would not be possible without you!

Doug Walsh: This guide would not have been possible without the talented people at Epic who opened their doors and invited me into their world for two weeks. I especially want to thank each of the following Epic employees whose support, suggestions, and hospitality were greatly appreciated: Cliff Bleszinski, Rod Fergusson, Jerry O'Flaherty, Josh Jay, Scott Bigwood, Preston Thorne, Mikey Spano, Maury Mountain, Aaron Smith, and Chris Bartlett. Whether it was answering random questions about the game, providing assets, guaranteeing me a coveted seat in the daily multiplayer sessions, or by drawing the fantastic-looking maps that appear throughout this guide, your contributions were vital, and I thank you. Of course, I would have never had the opportunity to author this book if not for Leigh Davis, Tim Fitzpatrick, Mike Degler, and David Waybright at BradyGames thinking me a good candidate for the job. I was thrilled to learn of this assignment back in May, and I'm happy to say that my excitement was justified—*Gears of War* was as fun as I hoped it would be. And speaking of fun, this book definitely benefits from the hard work of Jim Morey, who worked tirelessly to assist me in creating the book's Co-Op and Multiplayer chapters—may your Mets win it all this year! Lastly, I want to thank my loving wife, Kristin, whose constant encouragement and support is more appreciated than she'll ever know. I love you, baby!

PHIL COLE **Hometown:** Fresno, CA

The most challenging aspect of working on this level was getting the pacing right and making sure that it works as well in co-op as it does in single-player. We started with an abandoned factory at night in the rain and, on top of that, layered split-second glimpses of enemies that don't initially attack you and noises and groans around every corner. You're always on edge waiting for the attack to happen, so the suspense builds until the combat is finally sprung on you. You can build suspense only for so long before it starts to fall apart. If you never follow through on the threat of an attack, players stop believing they are in danger and they stop taking the threats seriously.

IMULSION MINES

WARREN MARSHALL **Hometown:** Hamilton, ON Canada

The Imulsion Mines is an interesting level because you're heading underground into enemy territory. You're meeting the enemy on their home turf, and that's pretty intimidating. Don't be afraid to look around a little, as there are nooks and crannies everywhere, and some of them might hold useful stuff. By the way, if you haven't learned to deal with Dark Wretches yet, you're going to get a quick education!

EAST BARRICADE ACADEMY

PAUL MADER **Hometown:** Karlskron, Germany

East Barricade Academy was one of the first *Gears of War* maps shown in early video footage. I was amazed how good it looked at that time but, still, it's great to see how much the map improved since then and how it turned out in the end. Nearly all of the Locust Horde units are represented in this area, and the wide courtyards give you the possibility to fight the enemy any way you want. The enemy variety and overwhelming numbers make it a very challenging experience you don't want to miss. It is a big part of the game, and everybody who worked on this map did an amazing job. I am glad to be a part of it.

EPHYRA STREETS

SIDNEY RAUCHBERGER **Hometown:** Hamburg, Germany

In Ephyra Streets, you get to take command over Delta Squad for the first time. Here, you're in for some hardcore split battles. And throughout all of that, the Corpser is hunting you in the background, while the introduction of the Boomers serves to most definitely keep you on your toes. The biggest challenge in maintaining the level was to keep the feel of its wide-open nature consistent throughout most of its areas.

OLD EPHYRA

STU FITZSIMMONS **Hometown:** Peterborough, England

One of the goals for Old Ephyra was to switch up the style of play. At this point in the game, the player has seen a lot of combat and will probably be getting used to the dynamic of taking cover and flanking enemies. In Old Ephyra, we introduce the Kryll, which forces the player to also stay in the light. It's a good opportunity to make players think about the environment more and how they can use it to create a path or kill their enemy. It was also a great setup for going deeper into the "Stranded" and finding out who they are and how they live. Hopefully players will enjoy the change of pace.

VIADUCTS

RYAN BRUCKS **Hometown:** Vista, CA

In Viaducts, Marcus and Dom must navigate the Junker through the war torn streets of Old Ephyra to rendezvous with Gus and Baird. Broken sections of highway hang suspended among the rubble, and debris litters the streets. Worse, the Kryll have claimed these streets in the darkness, and the player's chance of survival lies in the one available powerful source of light: the UV Turret mounted atop the Junker. The Junker has only enough power to run the engine or the UV turret, so players must balance the need to drive on with the need to fend off Kryll attacks. Drive carefully and avoid debris to maintain your speed to escape the Kryll and rendezvous with the rest of Delta Squad.

ENIX ESTATE

VE SPALINSKI **Hometown:** Trenton, NJ

the time you reach the Fenix Estate,
've got your hands dirty enough with just
ut every weapon in the game. We decided
design the level around the idea that the
yer is probably feeling pretty bad-ass at
s point. We wanted to keep that sensation
ing, so we knew the scenario would need
lend itself to that. This is where the
cision for a siege on the main character's
ildhood home came from. The setting also
lps to ground the player and make him
alize that this world was once lived in and
red for. Once that thought sinks in, we
ce the player to defend the home like it
his very own. When the suicidal Boomer
stroys the front door and all the Locust
art rushing in, we want the player to be
ying, "Get out of my house!" One of the
ficult things about working on this level
s not making the cellar section longer. It's
dank and creepy that we wanted to do
ore with it. However, in the end we decided
t to lengthen it since the player has to
cktrack through the entirety of the cellar
er reaching the hidden lab, and we didn't
nt anyone to forget they were in a house.

YRO PILLAR

N SPENCER **Hometown:** Whittier, CA

working on Tyro Pillar, I wanted to convey
sense of urgency that would make players
l they were running out of time. The key
playing Tyro Pillar is weapon selection.
thin the level, the player has to fight a
iety of Locust types, some for the first
e. I recommend having one weapon for
g range up until the tunnel starts; the
quebow worked best for me. Once in
tunnel, switch to the Gnasher to make
ting the Dark Wretches a lot easier.
ile you may feel the urge to rush through
level, be sure to take your time, as
hing will only cause you to have to fight
re Locusts simultaneously.

EMBRY SQUARE

GRAYSON EDGE   **Hometown:** Dallas, Texas

We wanted to do something with a grand scale, something that immediately suggested space, mood, and depth. Embry Square was the capitol city of the COG (Coalition of Ordered Governments), and to define this region we looked toward French, English, Italian and North American cityscapes. In particular, we looked at structures in Washington DC, the architecture of the Palais Royal in France, and the infamous Pantheon. Our concept artist, John Wallin, also played a central role in defining Embry's unique look. The combat in the capitol city is primarily conducted in open spaces. This gives new players adequate room to move around, experiment, and acclimatize to the battle environment in *Gears of War*. We also wanted to teach people that they could quickly turn the tide of a battle by taking advantage of their enemy's flank. It is important to note that flanking is one of the key strategies in *Gears of War*.

HOUSE OF SOVEREIGNS

DAVE EWING   **Hometown:** Walkerton, ON Canada

In my opinion, House of Sovereigns will be remembered for two things: the majestic architecture and the frantic first fight in the wide-open courtyard in front of the building. Using the huge amount of cover to attack the machine gun nest provides a great showcase for the main gameplay mechanic of *Gears of War*—the use of cover to flank your opponents and negate their cover. I'd love to take credit for the level myself, however I was merely a caretaker for it during the final months, with Phil, Ryan, Grayson, and Ken all having much influence in its creation.

TOMB OF THE UNKNOWNS

ANDREW BAINS   **Hometown:** New Orleans, LA

The Tomb is where the player first encounters the Berserker. It's the first occasion in the game that requires the player to drastically change tactics. The gameplay isn't about taking cover and flanking. It's about walking quietly, strategically making noise in order to lure the Berserker, and diving to safety as she barrels toward you. The challenge was in communicating this new gameplay style to the player through the actions and responses of the Berserker. The credit goes to AI programmer Steve Superville for making the Berserker behave effectively. Fighting her is a blast—I've played the level a thousand times, but I still jump when the she plows through a couple of pillars and smashes me to bits!

GEARS OF WAR

THE MEN BEHIND THE LEVELS

Marcus, Dom, and the other COG soldiers, not to mention the menacing Locust Horde, aren't the only stars of *Gears of War*. A major source of the entertainment comes from the engaging and sophisticated environments that play host to the action. The level design for *Gears of War* was very much a collaborative effort. All the people spotlighted on these pages would be quick to tell you that they aren't solely responsible for any individual level and that each area in the game was the product of a team effort. That said, we couldn't pass up the chance to hear what the game's talented level designers have to say about their creations.

LEAD LEVEL DESIGNER
LEE PERRY   **Hometown:** Southlake, TX

For me, all the levels represent an attempt to give the player a very different experience with each new area. One of our major goals was to mix up the gameplay situations without abandoning the core combat that ties the experience together as a whole. We want the player to be familiar with the actions available to them, see them in a new context through the different areas, and find different uses for the skills they're developing…ultimately taking it online where the levels will allow combat to evolve in ways we can't foresee.

PRISON
DAVE NASH   **Hometown:** Los Angeles, CA

There were several design goals for the Prison level. For one, we wanted to create a level that was visually impressive. Since this is the first environment that the player would see in *Gears of War*, we had to make sure that the visual fidelity that our engine provides was on full display. We also wanted to teach the player the basics of the game. Since many players prefer to jump right into the action when they first load up a game, we decided to leave it up to them to choose how much training they received. We do this by allowing them to choose from two routes through the prison. If they choose the combat route, we teach them only the basic fundamentals: how to take cover, how to revive a downed buddy, and that kind of thing. Or they can choose to take the training route, which is a longer path through the prison that offers additional tutorials. The last goal of this introductory level—one which I feel we accomplished particularly well—was to make the training level feel like part of the rest of the game instead of being a disconnected "boot camp" scenario.

GEARS OF WAR